The Barrett Files: A Civil War Pension Case

The Original Transcribed Documents 1866-1921

Transcribed and Compiled by

Karen Yvonne Hamilton

2020

The Barrett Files: A Civil War Pension Case

The Original Transcribed Documents 1866-1921

Edited by Karen Yvonne Hamilton

© 2020 Yesterday Press. All rights reserved.

Yesterday Press

www.yesterdaypress.com

Jupiter, Florida

Cover Design: Karen Yvonne Hamilton

ISBN: 978-1-7347858-1-4

FORWARD

In 1866 Stephen Barrett filed for an arrearage of pay from his service with the Union Colored Troops during the Civil War. Ten years later he was dead, and his widow, Sarah, filed for a widow's pension. In a short time, Special Examiners discovered that the widow was not in fact ever married to Barrett. To complicate matters, another player arrived on the scene filing for a pension in the name of the dead soldier. This imposter, Richard Hamilton, was a notorious character from the Florida Everglades who had once been a slave in North Florida.

Hamilton created a drama that would later provide a score of legal documents that aided descendants of both families in learning important facts about their family history as well as providing them with the opportunity to 'hear' their ancestors speak through the depositions taken.

These documents are transcribed from copies of the original documents housed at the National Archives. The amazing thing about these documents is that, when laid out in chronological order like this, they tell a story, peopled with some fascinating characters. There is a beginning and an ending and many conflicts and plot twists throughout. The reader also comes away with a sense of the time period and the people who lived in the aftermath of the Civil War.

These documents were often illegible in places. Therefore, we have simply added an underscore ___ where it is impossible to infer what the word or name is. Spelling and grammar rules are preserved here as they appear in the documents. Words that we were able to infer from further research and through context are in parentheses.

Throughout the years, names are spelled differently by different examiners. For instance, 'Isom Anthony' is sometimes written 'Anthony Isom'. The town of Killona in Louisiana is spelled 'Kelona' 'Killona' and 'Kilona'. We have preserved the spellings as they appear on the original document. At this writing, we have yet to research these individuals to determine the correct spelling.

Richard Hamilton (alias Stephen Barrett

Table of Contents

List of Examiners, Deponents, and Witnesses _____ 1
Discharged Stephen Barrett _____ 6
Difference of Pay and Bounty _____ 8
DECLARATION FOR INVALID PENSION _____ 12
DECLARATION FOR INVALID PENSION _____ 18
DECLARATION FOR WIDOW'S PENSION. _____ 21
Official character as a Justice of the Peace of Jose de Lamar _____ 23
Request for Doctor Examination _____ 24
Medical Examination Ordered _____ 25
Surgeon's Certificate _____ 26
GENERAL AFFIDAVIT. _____ 30
Inquiry Slip _____ 31
Canady deceased _____ 32
Transfer of Attorneyship _____ 34
Is the soldier dead? _____ 35
Request for soldier's records _____ 36
Intermittent Fever _____ 37
Attorney filed claim with Pension Bureau _____ 38
Transfer from Bushall to Kurtz _____ 39
DEPOSITION A Sarah Barrett _____ 40
DEPOSITION B Isom Anthony _____ 44
DEPOSITION C Mary T. Dominique _____ 46
Her relations with the soldier were entirely adulterous _____ 49
Dupart-Barnett Case _____ 51
LIST OF OFFICERS AND COMRADES _____ 53
Furnish full list of surviving members of regiment _ 55
The Key West man is an imposter _____ 57
Contesting Claims _____ 59
Regarding Deposition of James Dean _____ 61
Undated note _____ 63
Claimant can't be found _____ 64

Claimant might be located.	66
DEPOSITION A James Dean (Gilpin)	68
Richard Hamilton's Whereabouts	71
Claimant located	72
DEPOSITION A Nelson F. English	73
DEPOSITION B Joseph Pinkney	76
DECLARATION FOR WIDOW'S PENSION.	79
AFFIDAVIT William Martin & Nelson Whitehead	83
Affidavit William Martin & Nelson Whitehead	85
Affidavit Isam Anthony & Paul Cooper	87
Barrett alias Hamilton	89
Peculiar, Lawless, Desperate Character	94
Letter of Rejected Claim to Richard Hamilton	98
Summary of Sarah Barrett Case	100
DEPOSITION B Nelson Whitehead	107
DEPOSITION D Milton S. Cox	112
DEPOSITION A Sarah Barrett	117
DEPOSITION A cont. Sarah Barrett	121
DEPOSITION C Isham Reed	123
DEPOSITION E John Miller	127
Recommend reference to Law Division	130
Law Division - No further action necessary	135
CLAIM FOR BOUNTY, ARREARS OF PAY, ETC.	136
Letter to J.M. Phipps	139
Request for names of soldiers in Co. G	141
List of soldiers serving in Co. G	142
Exhibit C.	142
"a very stupid and ignorant negro"	146
Exhibit B	149
Letter to Everglades Postmaster	150
Letter to Stephen Barrett alias Richard Hamilton	151
Letter from Richard Hamilton to J A Davis	153
"One thing I will add that you have not asked for"	154
Criminal Work	156

DEPOSITION D Richard Hamilton	158
DEPOSITION O Stephen Barrett alias Richard Hamilton	166
DEPOSITION F Nathan H. DeCoster	169
DEPOSITION G A. Judson Edwards	171
DEPOSITION E Richard Hamilton	174
DEPOSITION L J. M. Phipps	179
DEPOSITION M George G. Brooks	181
DEPOSITION N F. W. Johnson	184
DEPOSITION H Ellick Anderson	186
DEPOSITION I Joseph Edwards	188
DEPOSITION K Henrietta E. Jones	190
Exhibit S, Letter to E. R. Pasley	193
"foul murder has been done by him"	194
Letter to Thomasville, GA Postmaster Regarding Robert Leggins and Louis Bennet (colored)	196
Thomas Hamilton	197
Recommend criminal proceedings	198
Summary of Depositions	200
Accused is indicted	213
Treasury Department	215
APPENDIX	220

List of Examiners, Deponents, and Witnesses

Names are not in order of appearance; they are listed in alphabetical order. Names of people who simply witnessed signatures (not actually witnesses in the case) have been excluded.

SPECIAL EXAMINERS

George M. Beckett, Special Examiner of the Pension Office

J. A. Davis, Special Examiner of the Pension Office, Jacksonville, Florida

C.M. Gilpin (Gilkin), Special Examiner of the Pension Office, Newberne, North Carolina

J. W. Montgomery, Special Examiner of the Pension Office, New Orleans, Louisiana

E. C. Wiggenhorn, Special Examiner of the Pension Office

Washington, D.C.

Frank E. (Anderson), Chief of Law Division

W. P. Canady

Hon. H. Clay Evans, Commissioner of Pensions

S. A. Cuddy, Chief of Law Division

T. (Stobo) Farror, Auditor

Fletcher, Chief of Law Division

Hon. William Lochren (Lockorn), Commissioner of Pensions

Joseph N. Stripling, Esq., U. S. Attorney

C. S. Bundy, Attorney for Stephen Barrett

Louisiana

Isom Anthony (also mentioned as Anthony Isom) Witness, Killona, St. Charles Parish

Sarah Barrett, Killona (Kelona), St. Charles Parish

Stephen Barrett, Algiers, Parish of Orleans

B. Boggs, Provost Marshal, St Charles Parish

Milton S. Cox, Witness, farmer, Hahnville

H. G. Crickmore, Witness, New Orleans

Mary T. Dominique, Witness, New Orleans

C. L. Ferguson, Witness, New Orleans

McKensie Griffin, Witness, New Orleans

Perry Jefferson, Witness, New Orleans

S. Magner, Notary Public, New Orleans

J. B. Martin, Clerk of the Court, St Charles Parish

William Martin, Witness, Hahnville

John Miller, (son of Sam Miller) LaPlace, St. John the Baptist Parish

Sam Miller, deceased, 2nd husband of Sarah Barrett

Thos. J. Myers, Notary Public, New Orleans

Isham Reed, Witness, "too old to work", Sellers, St Charles Parish

Colonel Peter Whitehead, Waterford Plantation, St. John Parish

Nelson Whitehead, Witness, Hahnville

North Carolina

James Dean, Witness, Minister of the Colored Methodist Church at Newberne, former Sub Agent for W.P. Canady

C. M. Gilpin, Special Examiner, Newberne

Florida

Andrew Anderson, Witness

Ellick Anderson, Witness, Elmwood, Marion County

George G. Brooks, Attorney at Law, Key West

P. W. Bryant, Inspector in the Custom House at Key West. Postmaster, the City Marshall, City Clerk in charge of registration lists

Nathan H. DeCoster, fruit grower, Harbor View, DeSoto County

Joseph N. Edwards, farmer, Williston, Levy County

A. Judson Edwards, farmer and stock raiser, Ocala, Marion County

Nelson English, ex postmaster

Richard Hamilton (Robert Hamilton, alias Stephen Barrett), Key West & Everglades

Thomas Hamilton, Sarasota

Captain Frank Hardings, Company C, 99 Regiment of US Colored Infantry, Tallahassee

F. W. Johnson, Officer Dep U.S. Marshal, Key West

Henrietta Edwards Jones, Williston, Levy County

Hannah Elizabeth Moore (Moore) McCloud

James A. Roberts, ex-sheriff

J. M. Phipps, Notary Public, Key West

Dr. E. R. , Williston

G. H. Watson, Everglade

Samuel J. Wellters Jr., Witness, Key West

Discharged Stephen Barrett

April 23, 1866 Tallahassee, Fla

To all whom it may Concern

KNOW YE, that Stephen Barrett, a Private of Captain Frank Hardings, Company C, 99 Regiment of US Colored Infantry, VOLUNTEERS, who was enrolled on the twentieth day of August one thousand eight hundred and sixty three to serve three years or during the war is hereby DISCHARGED from the service of the United States this 23 day of April, 1866, at Tallahassee, Fla by reason of service being no longer required No objection to his being reenlisted is known to exist.

Said Stephen Barrett was born in the State of Virginia, is twenty-five years of age, five feet six inches high, black complexion, black eyes, black hair, and by occupation; when enrolled, a laborer.

Given at Tallahassee, Fla this 23 day of April 1866.

                    Frank D. Hardings, Captain
                        Commanding the Reg't.

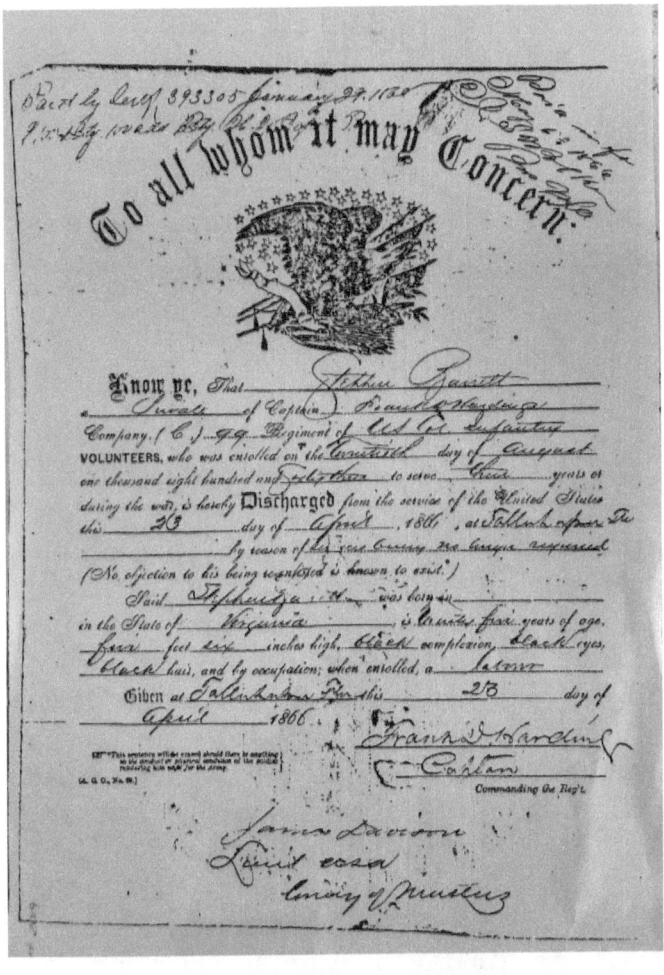

Difference of Pay and Bounty

November 13, 1866 New Orleans, Louisiana

Claim of Private Non-Commissioned Officer (Colored) for Difference of Pay and Bounty

State of Louisiana,
Parish of Orleans.

ON THIS 13 day of November, 1866, before me, a Notary Public in and for the Parish and State above named, personally appeared Stephen Barrett, aged 28 years, who being duly sworn according to law, declared that his residence and post-office address is Algiers, Parish of Orleans, R B, in the State of Louisiana that he is the identical Stephen Barrett who was a Private of Company C commanded by Captain Frank Hardings in the 99 Regiment of U. S. Colored Infantry volunteers. That he volunteered at New Orleans, La., on or about the 20 day of August 1863 for the term of 3 years and was honorably discharged at Tallahassee, Fla. on or about the 23 day of April, 1866, by reason of services being no longer required that a difference of pay is due him for services as aforesaid from the 20th day of August 1863, to the 1 day of May, 1864, which claim is based upon the fact that he was paid at the rate of seven dollars per month only, whereas, by law he was entitled to thirteen dollars per month pay, besides clothing allowance; also Bounty under Act approved 15th June, 1866.

Deponent further swears, he has not received nor authorized anyone to receive the Bounty due him under Act June 15th, 1866, except as hereinafter stated; that he has received no bounty on account of the services above stated, that the above is a true statement of all military service performed by him. And the said Stephen Barrett being further duly sworn deposes and says that he has not bartered, sold, assigned, transferred, loaned, exchanged, or given away his final discharge papers, or any interest in the Bounty provided for by an Act of Congress or by any regulation or order of the War Department.

He makes this declaration for the purpose of obtaining the Arrears of Pay, Extra Pay, Bounty Money, and all other arrearages and sums of money due him by reason of the services above stated; and he hereby constitutes and appoints C. S. Bundy & Co., Washington, D. of C. his Attorney, to prosecute this claim, and authorizes him to receive and receipt for a Draft, payable to this deponent's order, or to bearer, for whatever sum may be allowed on the same; and to do any other act or thing necessary to that end, the same as he might himself do if personally present, and revokes and countermands all former authority that may have been given for the above-specified purpose.

his
Stephen X Barrett
mark

In Presence of
    H. G. Crickmore
    C. L. Ferguson

Sworn to and subscribed before me, the day and year first above written; and on the same day personally came McKensie Griffin and Perry Jefferson, residents of New Orleans, La., who being duly sworn according to law, declare that they are personally acquainted with Stephen Barrett who has made and subscribed the foregoing declaration in their presence, and that he is the identical person who performed the service therein named, and that their knowledge of his identity is derived from Military service in the same regiment and Brigade. That they are disinterested in this claim and reside in the place above named.

his
McKensie X Griffin
mark

his
Perry X Jefferson
mark

In Presence of
    H. G. Crickmore
    C. L. Ferguson.

Sworn to and subscribed before me; and I certify that I believe the affiants to be credible persons; that the declarant is the person he represents himself to be, and further that I have no interest, direct or indirect, in this claim.

S. Magner, Not. pub.

I certify, upon oath, that C. S. Bundy & Co. have no other interest in the bounty claim of Stephen Barrett, late a Private of Co. C, 99 Reg't U. S. Colored Troops, than the legal fees allowed by the joint resolution of Congress approved July 26, 1866, and the expenses for notarial or other acknowledgments advance by us.

C. S. Bundy.

Sworn and subscribed to before me this 5 day of Decbr., 1866.

Thos. J. Myers,
Notary Public

DECLARATION FOR INVALID PENSION

January 19, 1891 Monroe County, Florida

Act of June 27, 1890

NOTE.-This can be executed before any officer authorized to administer oaths for general purposes. If such officer uses a seal, certificate of Clerk of Court is not necessary. If no seal is used, then such certificate must be attached.

State of Florida County of Monroe SS:

ON THIS 19th day of January, A. D. one thousand eight hundred and ninety one personally appeared before me, a Justice of the Peace within and for the County and State aforesaid Stephen Barrett aged forty-eight years a resident of the town of Key West County of Monroe, State of Fla., who, being duly sworn according to law, declares that he is the identical person who was *ENROLLED* on the (blank) day of (blank), 18__, in Private C. G. 99" La. in the war of the rebellion, and served at least ninety days, and was *Honorably Discharged* at Tallahassee on the (blank) day of (blank), 1865. That he is (partial) unable to earn a support by manual labor by reason of Rupture incurred in 186-- at (Natural) Bridge Fla.

That said disabilities are not due to his vicious habits and are to the best of his knowledge and belief permanent. That he has ___ applied for pension under application No (blank). That he makes this declaration for the purpose of being placed on the pension roll of the United States under the provisions of the Act of June 27, 1890. He hereby appoints W. P. CANADAY & CO., WASHINGTON, D. D. his true and lawful attorneys to prosecute his claim, and he directs that the sum of ten dollars be paid them for their services.

That his POST OFFICE ADDRESS is ℅ Jas Dean, Key West County of Monroe State of Fla.

	his
James Dean	Stephen X Barrett
	mark

Andrew Anderson
Two witnesses who can write, sign here.

Also personally appeared James Dean residing at Key West and Andrew Anderson, residing at Key West, persons who I certify to be respectable and entitled to credit, and who, being by me duly sworn, say they were present and saw Stephen Barrett, the claimant, sign his name or make his mark to the foregoing declaration; that they have every reason to believe from the appearance of said claimant and their acquaintance with him for three years and fourteen years, respectively, that he is the identical person he represents himself to be; and that they have no interest in the prosecution of this claim.

James Dean
Andrew Anderson

Sworn to and subscribed before me this 19th day of January, A. D. 1891 and I hereby certify that the contents of the above declaration, &c., were fully made known and explained to the applicant and witnesses before swearing, including the words (blank) erased, and the words (blank) added, and that I have no interest, direct or indirect, in the prosecution of this claim.

Jose de Lamar
Official Signature
Justice of the Peace
Official Character.

The Act of June 27, 1890, *requires*, in case of a soldier:

1. An honorable discharge, but the certificate need not be filed unless called for.
2. A minimum service of ninety days.
3. A permanent physical disability not due to vicious habits. It need not have originated in the service.
4. The rates under the act are graded from $6 to $12, proportioned to the degree of inability to earn a support, and are not affected by the rank held.
5. A pensioner under prior laws may apply under this one, or a pensioner under this one may apply under other laws, but he cannot draw more than ONE pension for the same period.

SOLDIERS APPLICATION.

Act of June 27, 1890.

Name *Stephen Garrett*

Service *[illegible]*

Address *Key West, Fla.*

laws, but he cannot draw more than ONE pension for the same period.

Filed by

W. P. CANADAY & CO.,

712 10th St., N. W.,

Washington, - - - D. C.

Printed and for sale by W. P. Canaday & Co.

No claim on new record Mar. 3/91

INQUIRY SLIP.

FROM

W. P. Canaday & Co.

TO THE

PENSION BUREAU.

June 5 - 91.

Application No. 996,454

Certificate No.

NAME OF SOLDIER.

Stephen Barrett

Co. G 99" Reg't. La Vols

INFORMATION DESIRED:

We would respectfully request that an examination order be issued in the above case,

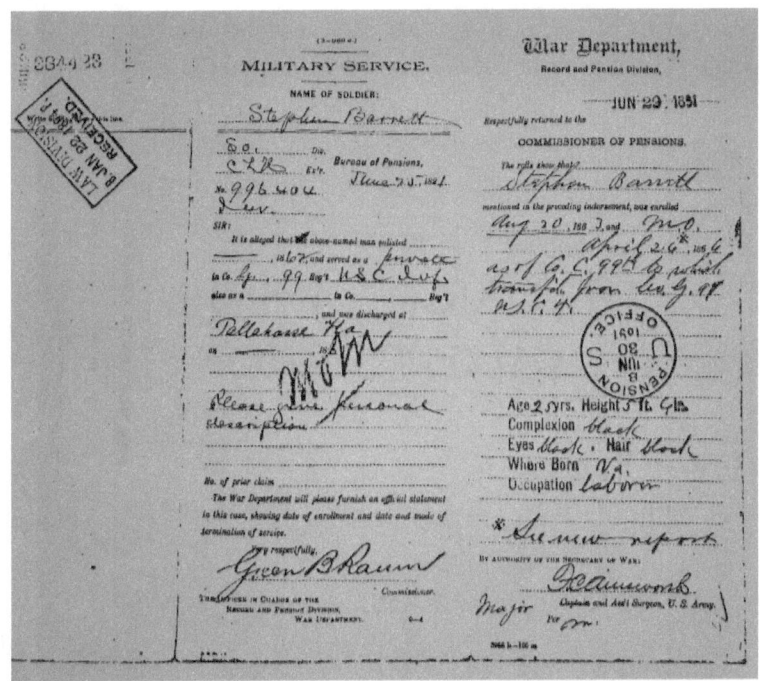

EDITOR'S NOTE: In January 1891, Stephen Barrett was 48 years old. Nine months later, in an additional declaration, he was listed as 61 years old. The rest of the information in these two declarations are mostly exactly the same except for this 13-year age difference.

DECLARATION FOR INVALID PENSION

October 9, 1891 Monroe County, Florida

Acts of June 27, 1890, and May 9, 1900.

NOTICE--This application may be sworn to before a JUSTICE OF THE PEACE, NOTARY PUBLIC, or before a Clerk of Court.

State of Florida, County of Monroe, ss:

ON THIS 9th day of October, A. D one thousand nine hundred and one personally appeared before me, J.M. Phipps, Notary Public within and for the County and State aforesaid, Stephen Barrett aged 61 years, a resident of the (blank), County of Monroe, State of Florida, who being duly sworn according to law, declares that he is the identical person who was *enrolled* on the (blank) day of (blank), 1862, in Co. G. 99 Louisiana as a private at Pleasunth Hill, Louisiana in the service of the United States in the War of the Rebellion, and served at least ninety days and was honorably discharged at Tallahassee, Florida, on the (blank) day of (blank), 1865.

That he has not been employed in the Military or Naval service otherwise than as stated above.

That he is partly unable to earn a support by manual labor by reason of rupture in the ___, that said rupture was incurred while engaged in the battle at Natural Bridge, Florida.

That said disabilities are not due to his vicious habits and are to the best of his knowledge and belief permanent. That he has applied for pension under Application No. (blank).

That he makes this declaration for the purpose of being placed on the pension-roll of the United States under the provisions of the Act of June 27, 1890, and under Act of May 9, 1900.

He hereby appoints, with full power of substitution and revocation HARVEY SPALDING & SONS, of WASHINGTON, D. C., his true and lawful attorneys to prosecute his claim, and to receive therefor a fee of TEN dollars; that his Post Office address is Everglade, County of Monroe, State of Florida.

ATTEST:	his
A W (Tolinson)	Stephen X Barrett
Geo. Brooks	mark

Two witnesses who write sign here

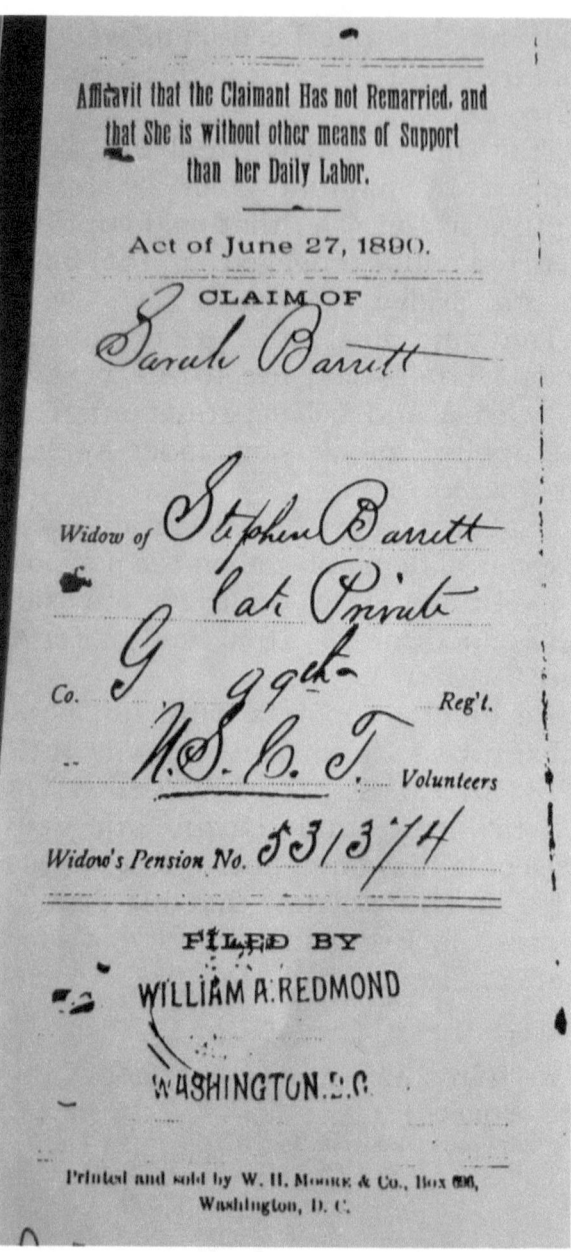

ACT OF JUNE 27, 1890.

DECLARATION FOR WIDOW'S PENSION.

October 28, 1891 New Orleans, Louisiana

To be executed before a Notary Public, Justice of the Peace, or any officer competent to administer oaths who has a Seal.

State of Louisiana, County of Orleans, ss:

On this 28th day of October, A. D., one thousand eight hundred and ninety-one, personally appeared before me, William B. Barnett, a Notary Public within and for the county and State aforesaid Sarah Barrett, aged 52 years, a resident of Waterford, county of St Charles, State of Louisiana, who, being duly sworn according to law, declares that she is the widow of Stephen Barrett, who enlisted under the name of Stephen Barrett at New Orleans, on the the 27th day of August A. D. 1863, in Co G. 99th U.S.C.T. as a Private and served at least ninety days in the late War of the Rebellion, who was HONORABLY DISCHARGED April 23rd 1866, and died in the month of March, 1886.

That she was married under the name of Sarah Miller, to said Stephen Barrett, on the (blank) day of (blank) 1880, by Rev. (blank), at St Charles Parish there being no legal barrier to said marriage.

That she has not remarried since the death of the said Stephen Barrett.

That she is without other means of support than her daily labor. That names and dates of birth of all the children now living under sixteen years of age of the soldier are as follows:
(none listed)

That she has heretofore applied for pension roll of the United States under the provisions of the Act of June 27, 1890.

She hereby appoints with full power of substitution and revocation, William A. Redmond, of Washington D. C. her true and lawful attorney to prosecute her claim, the fee to be TEN DOLLARS as prescribed by law. That her post-office address is Waterford P. O., County of St Charles, State of Louisiana.

	her
M T Dominique	Sarah X Barrett
Charles Lewis	mark
Two witnesses who write sign here	

===

EDITOR'S NOTE: In Sarah Barrett's widow's claim above, we find out that the real Stephen Barrett died in 1866, making the two 1891 declarations for pension highly suspect.

===

Department of the Interior,
BUREAU OF PENSIONS,

Official character as a Justice of the Peace of Jose de Lamar

Nov 2, 1891 Washington, D. C.

Sir,

In the claim for original invalid pension of Stephen Barrett, No. 996404 the genuineness of the signature, and the official character as a Justice of the Peace on June 26, 1891, of Jose de Lamar, County of Monroe and State of Florida, should be certified by the Clerk of the county or court of record or other proper officer under the seal of such county court or public officer, which should be in form of the blank at the foot hereof, that it may be placed on file for future reference, so that all persons filing papers executed before him during his term of office may refer thereto, and thus obviate the necessity of filing a certificate in each case.

This circular should be returned with your response.

Very respectfully,
___ B Ra___, Commissioner.

W. P. Canaday & Co.

Request for Doctor Examination

Nov 13, 1891

Department of the Interior,

BUREAU OF PENSIONS,

Nature of Claim original

No 996 404

Soldier: Steph. Barrett

Service: G 99 USCT

It is desired in this case that the examination be made with special reference to-

Rupture-

    Please describe the Hernia if you find it as alleged, and state the kind, and whether if ___it passes through both internal and external rings (?) and whether or not it is easily retained by a trust.

    Note any other disability you find after (successful) examination.

Thomas D. Ingram

Medical Examination Ordered

Nov 21, 1891

No. 996404

Name, Barrett

Co. G, 99 Reg't, USCY.

CHIEF BOARD OF REVIEW:

Medical examination has been ordered by me in this case to-day. Please see indorsement on jacket.

THOMAS D. INGRAM,
Medical Referee.

Nov. 21, 1891.

Surgeon's Certificate

Dec 23, 1891 Key West Florida

(3-111d.)

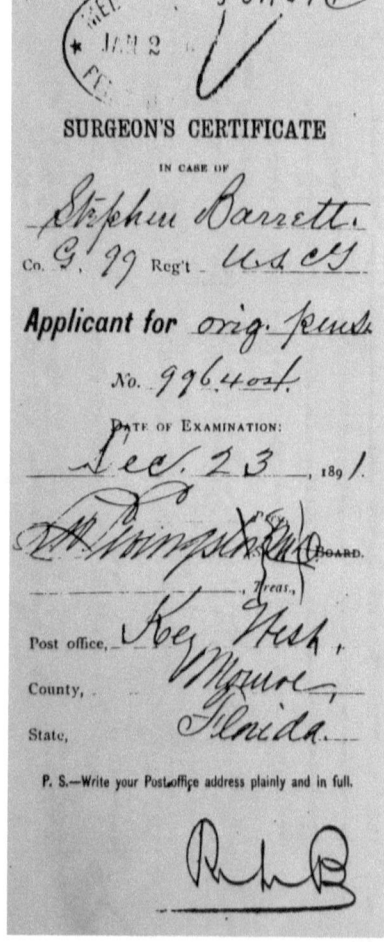

Attention is invited to the outlines of the human skeleton and figure upon the back of this certificate, and they should be used whenever it is possible to indicate precisely the location of a disease or injury, the entrance and exit of a missile, an amputation, &c.

The absence of a member from a session of a board and the reason therefor, (sic) if known, and the name of the absentee, must be indorsed (sic) upon each certificate.

(State always whether for original, ____, or restoration)

Original Pension Claim No. 996, 404

Stephen Barrett, rank, Private. Company "G" 99th Reg't U.S.C.T.

(___address of the Board) Key West, Fla. State, Key West, Fla

(Date of examination) Dec. 23, 1891.

I hereby certify that in compliance with the requirements of the law I have carefully examined this applicant, who states that he is suffering from the following disability, incurred in the service, viz
Hernia

He makes the following statement upon which he bases his claim for (Original, increase, restoration, &c.) original

That he was ruptured as a result of a heavy march to the relief of his regiment at Natural Bridge, near Tallahassee, Florida, in 1864; that the hernia came down suddenly and has been gradually growing worse; that it pains him considerably every now and again and is made worse by the hard labor he is compelled to do to earn his _____. (see margin note)

Upon examination we find the following objective conditions: Pulse rate, 75; respiration 21; temperature 98/4; height, 6 feet no inches; weight 154 pounds; age, 52 years.

This claimant has a reducible incomplete (does not pass external ring) right oblique _____ hernia.

He did not wear a truss but I think the hernia could be easily retained and would be much improved by wearing one.

No other disability was found to exist.

Written in the margin

(Statement continued) living; that it commenced as a lump and gradually increased in size but has never entered the ____; that he attempted to wear a truss but it chafed him so much he had to discard it; that when the hernia pains him he has pains also in the lower parts of the back and stomach; that otherwise his health is good.

He is, in my opinion, entitled to a 8/18 rating for the disability caused by Rupture ____

Signed ____

N. B. -Always forward a certificate of examination whether a disability is found ____

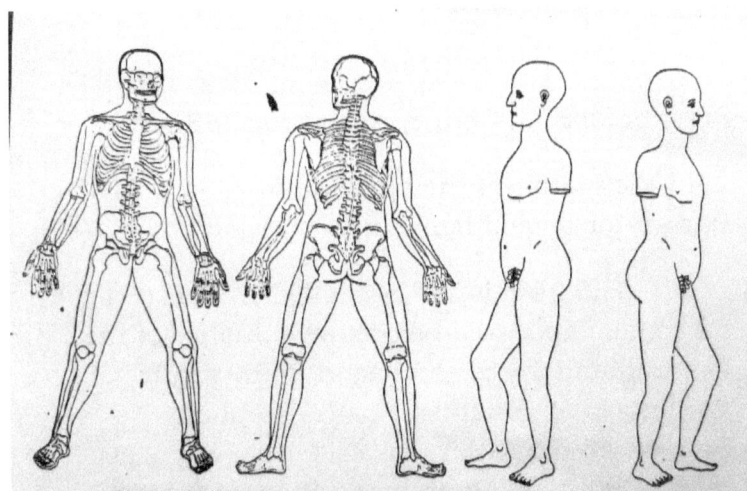

Single surgeons will use this blank, changing "we" to read "I," and "our" to read "my." They will erase the words "Pres.," "Sec'y," "Treas.," and "Board" where the words appear, and sign at the foot of the certificate, and also on the back of the same.

PROVIDED FURTHER, That all examinations shall be thorough and searching, and the certificate contain a full description of the physical condition of the claimant at the time, which shall include all the physical and rational signs and a statement of all the structural changes. [Extract from Section 4, Act of Congress approved July 25, 1882.]

GENERAL AFFIDAVIT.

December 26, 1891

State of Florida, County of Monroe,. SS:

In the matter of the application of Stephen Barrett for invalid Pension.

ON THIS 26th day of December A. D., 1891 personally appeared before me a Justice of the Peace in and for the aforesaid County duly authorized to administer oaths Stephen Barrett, aged 52 years, a resident of Key West, in the County of Monroe and State of Florida whose Post Office address is Key West Fla well known to me to be reputable and entitled to credit, and who being duly sworn, declared in relation to aforesaid case as follows:

That he has not been employed in the United Military or Naval since 1865 at which time he was discharged.

(blank) further declare that he has interest in said case and is concerned in its prosecution.

James Dean

his
Stephen X Barrett
mark

Samuel _____

If Affiants sign by mark two witnesses who can write sign here.

Inquiry Slip

FROM

W. P. Canady

TO THE

PENSION BUREAU

June 30, 1892

Application No. 996,404
Certificate No.

NAME OF SOLDIER

Stephen Barrett
Co. "G" 99th *Reg't.* U.S.C.T.

INFORMATION DESIRED

An examination order in the above cited claim is respectfully requested at an early date

26th 1891

Canady deceased

Nov 7, 1892

CLAIM OF

Stephen Barrett

Co. "G" 99th *Reg't*. U.S.C.T.
Wid 536374

~~No~~ 996,404

FOR

Pension
Act of June 27, 1890.

Washington D. C.

Hon. Commissioner of Pensions.

Sir: -

Attention is ____ ____ agreement, and schedule of claims, as transferred to me by John C. Callahan, Collector of the estate of W. P. Canady, deceased, filed Nov 7, 1892

Respectfully,
A. M. Bushell

Bureau of Pensions.

Application No. 996404
Certificate No. _____

NAME OF SOLDIER,
Stephen Barrett
Co. D, 99" Reg't U.S.C.T.

INFORMATION DESIRED.

Action —
Note transfer
as filed —
Nov. 7 - 92
C. M. Bushell

NOTICE

OF

Transfer of Attorneyship.

No. 996,404

Name <u>Stephen Barrett</u>

Service <u>G 99 U. S. C. Inf.</u>

Notice is hereby given of a transfer to me from A. M. Bushell of the above cited claim.

The transfer is duly filed with the Law Division of the Bureau of Pensions.

       Very respectfully,

I.S. Kurtz,

    1213 N. Capitol St.,

Washington, Nov. 21, 1893.

Is the soldier dead?

January 26, 1893 Washington, D. C.

DEPARTMENT OF THE INTERIOR,
BUREAU OF PENSIONS
WASHINGTON, D. C.,

Claim 531.374 and Claim 996.404
Claimant, Sarah Barrett
Soldier, Stephen Barrett
Co. G, 99 Reg't U. S.

Respectfully returned to the chief of the Southern Division. Is the soldier dead? The soldier's application was filed January 27, 1891, but the widow swears and proves that he died in 1886. The soldier states in his declaration that he had previously applied for a pension! The joint_____ affidavit is not sufficiently definite to prove all the points necessary to establish in a widow's claims.

    Fletcher, Chief of ___ Division.

Request for soldier's records

January 13, 1894 Washington, D. C.

DEPARTMENT OF THE INTERIOR,
BUREAU OF PENSIONS
WASHINGTON, D. C.,

The Officer in Charge,
    Record and Pension Office,
        War Department.

Sir:

For use in the claim of Sarah Barrett, widow of Stephen Barrett, late private, Co. C, 99th U. S. C Vol. Inf., Widow's Orig. No. 531,374, please furnish the soldier's full military and medical history and a tracing of his signature.

Please return this letter and your former report, herewith enclosed, with your reply.

        Very respectfully,
        _____ Lockorn
            Commissioner.

Intermittent Fever
January 22, 1894

Record and Pension Office,
War Department.

Respectfully returned to the
Commissioner of Pensions.

Stephen Barrett *Co.* G. 99 *Reg't* USC Inf. *was enrolled* Aug 20, *1863, and* M. O.[1] Apr 23, *1866,* as of Co. C 99 USC Inf. To which trans Dec. 8, *1865.* Signs by mark. *From* enr, ~~186_~~, *to* M. O. ~~186_~~, *he held the rank of* pvt *and during that period the rolls show him present* ~~except as follows~~

The above regiment was also known as 15 Regt ___ and 5 Regt ___ ___ until Mch or Apl 64.
The medical records show him treated as follow:
As Stephen Barrett, Prl, Co. G. 99 U.S.C.T., Sept 5 to 7, 65, Intermittent Fever, ___ duty.
Nothing additional found.

BY AUTHORITY OF THE SECRETARY OF ___
 Colonel, U. S. Army, Chief of Office.
Washington, D. C.,
COMMISSIONER OF PENSIONS.

---

[1] Mustered Out

Attorney filed claim with Pension Bureau

February 27, 1894 Washington, D. C.

Treasury Department
Office of the Second Auditor
Washington, D. C.

The Commissioner of Pensions,

Washington, D. C.

Sir:

In answer to your letter of the 15th instant, you are informed that on Dec. 6, 1866, C. S. Bundy, attorney, Washington, D.C., filed a claim for bounty executed before S. Magner, a notary public, by Stephen Barrett, Co. C, 99 U. S. C. Troops. Signature by x mark. Residence of claimant, New Orleans, La.

Respectfully yours,
T. (Stobo) Farror
Auditor

Pension claim Wid. No. 531, 374.

Transfer from Bushall to Kurtz

March 17, 1894

INQUIRY SLIP
FROM
I.S. Kurtz
TO THE
PENSION BUREAU.

March 17, 1894

Application No. 996404
Certificate No.

NAME OF SOLDIER:

Stephen Barrett
Co. G 99 *Reg't* U.S.C.Inf.

INFORMATION DESIRED:

This claim is included in the General Transfer from A. M. Bushall to me, filed Nov. 20, 1893.

Please give status of claim.

Mrs. Ida S. Kurtz,
1218 North Capitol St.,
Washington, D. C.

DEPOSITION A
Sarah Barrett

July 18, 1895 Killona, La

DEPOSITION A

Case of Sarah Barrett No. 531374

On this 18 day of July, 1895, at Killona, County of St Charles, State of La, before me J.W. Montgomery, Special Examiner of the Pension Office, personally appeared Sarah Barrett, who, being by me first duly sworn to answer truly all interrogatories propounded to her during this Special Examination of aforesaid pension claim, deposes and says:

My age is about 48 years, a widow, residence and PO address, Killona, La.

I claim a pension as the widow of Steven (sic) Barrett who was a soldier during the late war but I do not know in what company and regiment. I only know his captain was Mr. Hopper who died in this parish about twenty years ago. I know Anthony Isom who was in the same regiment with my husband. I was (bred) and born in N.C. and came to this parish 12 years before the war. I first lived in St. John Parish and after the war came here. My first husband was named Sam Miller who I married during the war. I married him by license procured at

Saint Charles courthouse. *Claimant exhibits marriage certificate signed by B. Boggs. Provost marshal dated Dec 5, 1864 St Charles Parish La. No. 1209*

I lived with Sam Miller for thirteen years when he went off and took another woman and I went about my business. I waited one year and six months then I took up with Stephen Barrett and we lived together for nine years when he died. I was never divorced from my first husband Sam Miller. He is yet living somewhere in St John Parish. I was never regularly married to Stephen Barrett. We had no license and no preacher. Isom Anthony told me what regiment Stephen was in. I haven't his discharge certificate and I never saw it. His sister was keeping it and when she died the things were scattered and it was lost. I have not remarried with any man since Stephen died. I had George Brown for one month and three weeks after Stephen died. Brown took sick and went to the hospital and died. A woman named Mary came here to the quarter and put in a claim for (me). She said she was sent out by the Governor. I gave her the (rise) of three dollars. She wrote down everything and asked me who were Stephen's witnesses and I said Isom Anthony and I took her to his house. I also gave her the name of Spencer Smith. I did not give her the name of Paul Cooper. I never heard my husband speak of him. I did not go to New Orleans La. to put in a claim. I have been there once since the woman was here but I did not see her there. I never saw her anywhere except here. Isom Anthony, a man named Paul Cooper and I never went to New Orleans to see about my pension claim or to make out any papers.

Today was the first time I have ever taken an oath about my pension claim.

My husband, the soldier, never had any name but Stephen Barrett. He came here from Va. with his old master and Peter Whitehead. I don't know where he was enlisted but he was mustered out at New Orleans La. I guess Stephen was about 5 feet and a half high and was a stout man. He grew stout after the war. He was about 55 years old when he died, and he has been dead nine or ten years. I had it written down on a piece of paper, the only record I had, and I gave it to her, and she carried it off. I did not pay her three dollars in cash, but I gave her four bits and the balance in chickens. The woman was colored.

I do not know a man named Dupart living in New Orleans. I never saw the woman Mary until she came here to take my claim. She was a kind of pedler (sic).

I have heard read the foregoing and am correctly reported herein.

her
Sarah X Barrett
mark

Sworn to and subscribed before me this 18 day of July 1895, I certify that the contents were fully made known to deponent before signing.

           J. W. Montgomery
                Special Examiner.

DEPOSITION B
Isom Anthony

July 18, 1895 Killona, La

DEPOSITION B

Case of Sarah Barrett, No. 531374.

On this 18 day of July 1895, at Killona, County of St Charles State of La, before me J. A. Montgomery, a Special Examiner of the Pension Office, personally appeared Isom Anthony, who, being by me first duly sworn to answer truly all interrogatories propounded to him during this Special Examination of aforesaid pension claim, deposes and says: My age is about 50 years, a laborer, residence and P.O. address is Kellona, La.

I served during the late war in Co. H.C. 99 US Col Inf. There was a man named Stephen Barrett who belonged to Co G of the same regiment. I first met him in the service. I don't know where he came from; Don't know where he lived prior to the war. He looked to me like he was about 50 years old. He was one or two inches over five feet. He was just a little taller than I. (Deponent is 5 feet 5 inches ?)

He was a little darker than gingercake and would weigh about 150 when in the army. He was mustered out with the regiment at Greensville, La. and came here to St. Charles parish. He had no wife with him in the war. He got a woman named Sarah on the Waterford place, but I can't say whether they were married, he lived with her until he died. I can't tell just when he died and I did not see his dead body, I did not go to his funeral.

I was never a witness for this claimant. A woman from New Orleans La named Mary Dominique came here to my house and asked me if I knew Sarah Barrett and I told her yes. She was round taking up claims for soldiers. Taking up claims for soldiers I never at any time went to New Orleans to be a witness for Sarah Barrett. I don't know a man named Paul Cooper. I cannot write my name. I did not know that my name was used in this claim. I did not touch the pen to any paper in this claim. I don't know any other person round here who was in my regiment. I am positive that Sarah Barretts husband, named Stephen Barrett was in Co. G of the 99 regiment. I am correctly reported herein.

    Isom (his mark) Anthony (his mark)

Attest: Richard G? & Louis Segura?

Sworn to and subscribed before me this 18 day of July, 1895, and I certify that the contents were fully made known to deponent before signing.

    J.W. Montgomery

        Special Examiner.

DEPOSITION C
Mary T. Dominique

July 19, 1895 New Orleans

DEPOSITION C

Case of Sarah Barrett, No. 996404 (sic) (correction 531.374)

On this 19 day of July, 1895, at New Orleans, County Orleans, State of La, before me, J. W. Montgomery, a Special Examiner of the Pension Office, personally appeared Mary T. Dominique, who, being by me first duly sworn to answer truly all interrogatories propounded to her during this Special Examination of aforesaid pension claim, deposes and says: My age is 42 years, no present occupation, residence and PO address No. 1941 Perdido Street, this city.

The first time I ever saw the above named claimant was in St Charles parish this state about three or four years ago. I was selling notions through that parish. I was also recommending old soldiers and their witnesses to agents. I was not working for any particular person and I have never received any compensation for any work done. I recommended this claimant to Mr. J. G. Dupart . I prepared no paper for her. When I saw her in St Charles parish I asked her to come to New Orleans and I think she came down in a week or so. She stopped back of town somewhere, but I cannot say where. I took her to Mr. Dupart's office, corner Damien and Villere Sts. and a paper was written out there. I don't know whether it was a claim for a pension. I can't remember whether there was anyone with her. Some man unknown to me came for me and carried me to where she was and we went Dupart's office but whether the man accompanied us I am unable to say. I identify my signature signed as attesting and identifying witness to application now shown me filed in Pension Office Nov 6, 1891. I did not go anywhere to swear to this paper. Mr. Dupart said Sarah would have to get witnesses and come back. I know a man named Paul Cooper, living in St. Charles Parish but do not know his p.o. address. He was not present at Dupart's office. I know WB Barnett but was not sworn by him in this case. Her statement that she never met me in this city is untrue. I went with her from the Whitehead plantation to the house of Isom Anthony to learn in what company and regiment her husband served. I did not collect anything from her. She paid me for merchandise I sold her, part in money and part in chickens.

I have no interest in this claim. I am not related to the claimant and am correctly reported in this deposition.

                M. T. Dominique, Deponent.

Sworn to and subscribed before me this 19 day of July 1895, and I certify that the contents were fully made known to deponent before signing.

        JW Montgomery
            Special examiner.

Her relations with the soldier were entirely adulterous

New Orleans La. July 19, 1895

No. 531394 Sarah Barrett, widow Stephen Barrett, soldier G. 99 U.S. Col. Inf. Basis of Claim Act June 27 1890	Post office address Killona St Charles Co. La.
No 996404. Stephen Barrett. G. 99 U.S. Cl Basis of Claim. Act June 27 1890	Post office address CO Jas. Dean. Key West Monroe Co. Fla.

Hon. Commissioner of Pensions,

Washington, D.C

Sir I have the honor to return with my report of special investigations the papers in the claims above cited which were consolidated and referred to the S. E. Division for a special examination under instructions of Law Division letter dated February 12 1894 to determine whether the papers in the widow's claim were executed as they purport.

This is a Dupart-Barnett case and the usual practices were resorted to.

Criminal prosecution is barred by the statute of limitation.

In addition the claimant, even if the widow of the soldier of record has no title under any law for the reason that she has a prior lawful husband living from whom she was never divorced. Her relations with the soldier were entirely adulterous. I could find no member of the alleged soldier's organization by whom identity can be satisfactorily established. Isom Anthony, if is true, served in the same regiment but in a different company, he has no doubt of the identity of this claimants husband with the soldiers of record, but I recommend that a list of course be procured and that the claim be first sent to Monroe Co. Fla. for the invalid claimants statement and then it will in all probability have to be returned to this locality where a great many of the late members of the 99 regiment reside.

I am of the opinion the invalid claimant is a fraud and a special examination will best determine whether such is the fact.

    Very respectfully,
      J.W. Montgomery
      Special Examiner

Dupart-Barnett Case

July 19, 1895 New Orleans

No. 531374 Sarah Barrett, widow. Post office address Killano, St. Charles, C., La. Stephen Barrett, Soldier, G-99-U.S. Col. Inf. Basis of claim Act June 27, 1890

No. 996404 Stephen Barrett, G-99-U.S. Col. Inf. Post office address %James Dean, Key West, Monroe Co., Fla. Basis of claim Act June 27, 1890

> Hon. Commissioner of Pensions,
> Washington, D.C.

Sir:

I have the honor to return with my report of special investigations the papers in the claims above cited which were consolidated and referred to the S. E. Division for a special examination under instructions of Law Division letter dated February 12-1894 to determine whether the papers in the widow's claim were executed as they purport.

This is a Dupart-Barnett case and the usual practices were resorted to. Criminal prosecution is barred by the statute of limitation.

In addition, the claimant, even if the widow of the soldier of record has no title under any law for the reason that she has a prior lawful husband living from whom she was never divorced. Her relations with the soldier were entirely adulterous. I could find no member of the alleged soldier's organization by whom identity can be satisfactorily established. Isom Anthony, if is true, served in the same regiment but in a different company, he has no doubt of the identity of this claimants husband with the soldier of record, but I recommend that a list of course be procured and that the claim be first sent to Monroe Co. Fla. for the invalid claimant's statement and then it will in all probability have to be returned to this locality where a great many of the late members of the 99 regiment reside.

   I am of the opinion the invalid claimant is a fraud and a special examination will best determine whether such is the fact.[2]

               Very respectfully,
                  J. A. Montgomery,
                        Special Examiner

---

[2] (See appendix for explanation of Dupart-Barnett Case)

SPECIAL EXAMINATION DIVISION.

LIST OF OFFICERS AND COMRADES

July 31, 1895

Co. G. 99 Reg't USCInf.

FOR USE IN CLAIM
No. 531,374 Wid

Washington, D.C.,

For the information of the Special Examiner to whom this case has been referred for investigation, the accompanying list of officers and comrades who served in the same military organization with the claimant about whom inquiry is to be made, together with their last known post office addresses, is furnished. The Special Examiner will not confine his inquiries to this list of comrades but will seek out others if necessary.

Chief of Division.

Wid 531,374
Name Stephen Barrett

Co. G 99 Reg't USCInf.
P.O. Dead
Enlisted Aug 20 1863
Discharged Apr 26 1866

>Department of the Interior,
>BUREAU OF PENSIONS.
>Washington, D. C.

Chief Army and Navy Survivors Division:

Please furnish the names and P. O. addresses of officers and Staff comrades of Co. G. 99. Reg't USCInf for use in above case.

Furnish full list of surviving members of regiment

July 31, 1895 Washington, D. C.

Department of the Interior,
Bureau of Pensions,
Washington, D. C.

To the Chief of the A. N. S. Division.

Sir:

For use during a pending investigation of the contesting claims of Sarah Barrett, No. 531, 374, and Stephen Barrett, late of Co. G, 99th U. S. C. V. I., No. 999,404, (enlisted August 20, 1863, and discharged April 26, 1866), you are requested to furnish a full list of the post office addresses of the surviving members of the company and of the staff officers of the regiment.

Please return this letter with your reply.

Very respectfully,
Chief of Law Division

EDITOR'S NOTE: The document dated Nov 4 1897 calls for a correction to reports stating that Barrett was transferred from Company G to Company C (date of transfer unknown), which explains the differing notes about the Company he served in.

SPECIAL EXAMINATION DIV.

Fd. 537,374
Name: Stephen Barrett
Co: G 99 U.S.C. Inf
P: Dead
Enlisted: Aug. 20 - '63
Discharge: Apl 26 - '66

Department of the Interior,
BUREAU OF PENSIONS.

Washington, D.C., July 31, 1895

Chief Army and Navy Survivors' Division:

Please furnish the names and P.O. addresses of officers and **Staff** comrades of Co. G 99 Reg USC Inf for use in above case.

_____
Chief Special Examination Division.

NAME	RANK	PRESENT P.O. ADDRESS
Uri B. Pearsall	Lt Col & Bvt	Bourbon Co. Kans.
Rudolph B. Baquie	Sg/Maj	136 Berlin St. New Orleans La.
Orr J Smalley	1st R.Q.M.	143-10 St. St. Paul Minn
Arthur Thompson	Sg/Maj	Brooksville Hernando Co. Fla
Walter H. Hutchinson	1st Lt.	Bristol - Hartford Ct.
Robert Liggins	Cor.	Thomasville Thomas Co. Ga.
Louis Bennett		

Respectfully returned to Chief Special Examination Division with the desired information as far as known.

July 31, 1895

S. W. Roberts
Chief Army and Navy Survivors' Division.

The Key West man is an imposter

August 2, 1895 Washington, D. C.

Law Division
Department of Interior,
Bureau of Pensions,
Washington, D. C.

Chief of the
  Special Examination Division.

Sir:

Herewith are forwarded the papers in the contesting claims of Stephen Barrett, of Key West, Monroe Co., Florida, who claims to be the soldier of that name who served in Co. G, 99th U. S. C. V I. No 996,404, and of Sarah Barrett, of Killona, St. Charles Parish, La., who claims to be said soldier's widow, No. 531,374, together with a report of Special Examiner J. W. Montgomery, relative thereto.

Sarah Barrett had a living husband when she married the Stephen Barrett, whom she claims to have been the soldier who performed the service, and hence has no pensionable status, even if the Key West man is, as seems probable, an imposter.

As is shown by the records of the War Department, the soldier was twenty-five years of age and five feet, six inches in height, in 1863, and would be fifty-seven years of age, if living.

The invalid applicant, in his declaration, gives his age as forty-eight, in 1891, and the certificate of medical examination made in 1891 gives his height as six feet.

You are requested to forward the papers to a Special Examiner for further examination at Key West, Monroe Co., Florida, and such other places in the vicinity as may be necessary, for the purpose of determining whether the invalid applicant is the soldier who performed the service, or an imposter.

This letter should appear as an exhibit in the Examiner's report.[3]

        Very respectfully,
                Frank E. Anderson (sp?),
                      Chief of Law Division.

---

[3] Acting commissioner, H. C. Bell replied on Aug 6 with copies of the envelopes he addressed to Richard Hamilton in Key West and Cape Sable.

Contesting Claims

August 2, 1895 Washington, D. C.

Department of the Interior,
Bureau of Pensions,
Washington, D. C.

August 2, 1895.

Chief of the
Special Examination Division,

Sir:

Herewith are forwarded the papers and the contesting claims of Stephen Barrett, of Key West, Monroe County, Florida, who claims to be the soldier of that name who served in Co. G, 99th U. S. C. V. I. No. 996,404, and of Sarah Barrett, of Killona, St. Charles Parish, La., who claims to be said soldiers widow, No. 531,374, together with a report of special Examiner J. W. Montgomery, relative thereto.

Sarah Barrett had a living husband when she married the Stephen Barrett, whom she claims to have been the soldier who performed the service, and hence has no pensionable status, even if the Key West man is, as seems probable, an imposter.

As shown by the records of the war department, the soldier was 25 years of age and 5 ft, 6 in in height, in 1863, and would be 57 years of age, if living.

The invalid applicant, in his declaration, gives his age as 48, in 1891, and the certificate of medical examination made in 1891 gives his height as 6 ft.

You are requested to forward the papers to a special examiner for further examination at Key West, Monroe County, Florida, and such other places in the vicinity as may be necessary, for the purpose of determining whether the invalid applicant is the soldier who performed the service, or an imposter.

This letter should appear as an exhibit in the examiner's report.

        Very respectfully,
           Frank A. _____,
           Chief of Law Division

Regarding Deposition of James Dean

February 18th, 1896 Newberne, N. C.

Sir:

I have the honor to return all the papers in the claim number 531.37 for, Sarah Barrett, Widow of Steven Barrett, G, 99, U.S.C.T. whose post office address is Kelona St Charles County Louisiana also to return all the papers in the claim of Steven (sic) Barrett who alleges service in company G99, U.S.C.T., who's post office address is given as Key West, Monroe County, Florida, and to submit my report there on.

Claim was forwarded to obtain the deposition of James Dean, relative to the address of Steven (sic) Barrett, and identifying witness Andrew Anderson. The deposition of said Dean is submitted here with. He states that he has had no communication from the claimant for the last three years, neither does he know the whereabouts of Andrew Anderson, but thanks. Samuel J Wellters Jr. of Key West, Florida, would probably know of Barrett's whereabouts.

I recommend further examination at Key West, Florida. From the date embraced Indians statement I think the claimant might be located.

Very respectfully

C.M. Gilpin
Special Examiner.

Hon. William
Lochren, Com'r of Pensions, Washington, DC

Undated note

___ Sir in reply ___ that a colored man known as Richard Hamilton also as Robert E Hamilton resides near here has been living since married the _____ one under the name of Richard Hamilton wife ____ ____ name _____ Robert Hamilton has been indicted for bigamy in Monroe Co Fla claims to be Choctaw Indian descent. His first wife ___ a white woman the wife he has now is mixed Blood.

(signed)

Claimant can't be found

February 5, 1896 Key West

Hon. Commissioner of Pensions,
    Washington, D. C.

Sir:

I have the honor to return, herewith, without report, all the papers in contesting claims of Stephen Barrett, No. 996.404, who alleges service in Co. G. 99th U.S.C.V.I. and of Sarah Barrett, No. 531.374, who alleges she is the widow of Stephen Barrett, who served in Co. G. 99th U.S.C.V.I. together with report of Special Examiner, Montgomery, and Law Div, letter dated Aug. 2nd 1895, forwarding the papers with instructions.

I have made an extended and diligent search for the claimant, Stephen Barrett, at Key West, Fla, and have not been able to get the slightest clue.

I consulted with the Postmaster, the City Marshall, City Clerk, in charge of registration lists, a colored lawyer, P. W. Bryant, who was for twelve years an Inspector in the Custom House at Key West, Fla. Nelson English, (colored) ex postmaster, James A. Roberts (colored)Ex Sheriff and numerous others in all walks of life with whom I came in contact. No one appears to know the claimant or his identifying witness, Andrew Anderson[4].

The claimants address appears on the papers as, %James Dean, Key West, Fla. The latter was an alleged Atty at Law, left here with an unsavory reputation and is now said to be a Minister of the Colored Methodist Church at Newberne, N.C.

I respectfully suggest that the papers be forwarded to an Examiner in the Newberne, N.C. Dist for the purpose of obtaining from said Dean (if possible) the claimant's address and the whereabouts of Andrew Anderson, after which, such further examination as ___ __ ___.

    Very respectfully
    Your Obd. Svt.,
     J. A. Davis
     Special Examiner

---

[4] NOTE (KYH) Andrew Anderson would be the son of Lou Anderson and Peggy Hamilton (Richard's half brother).

Claimant might be located.

February 18, 1896 Newberne, N. C.

Sir:

I think the claimant might be located.

I have the honor to return all the papers in the claim No. 531374, Sarah Barrett, widow of Stephen Barrett, G. 99, U.S.C.T. who's post office address is Killona, St. Charles Co., La. also to return all the papers in the claim of Steven Barrett who alleges service in Co G. 99. U.S.C.T., whose post office address is given as Key West, Monroe Co, Fla., and to submit my report thereon.

Claim was forwarded to obtain the deposition of James Dean, relative to the address of Steven Barrett, and identifying witness Andrew Anderson. The deposition of said Dean is submitted herewith. He states that he has had no communication from the claimant for the last three years, neither does he know the whereabouts of Andrew Anderson, but thinks that Samuel J. Welters, Jr of Key West, Fla., would probably know of Barrett's whereabouts.

I recommend further examination at Key West, Fla. From the data embraced and Dean's statement I think the claimant might be located.

    Very respectfully,
    CM Gilpin

Special Examiner.

Hon. William Lochren,
     Com'r of Pensions,
          Washington, D. C.

DEPOSITION A
James Dean (Gilpin)

February 18, 1896 New Berne, Craven Co., N.C.

DEPOSITION A

Case of Stephen Barrett, No. 996.404

On this 18 day of Feb, 1896, at New Berne, County of Craven State of N.C. before me, C.M. Gilkin (sic), a Special Examiner of the Pension Office, personally appeared James Dean, who, being by me first duly sworn to answer truly all interrogatories propounded to him during this special examination of aforesaid pension claim, deposes and says:

I am 37 years old, occupation Minister, residence at post office address is New Berne N.C.

I formerly lived in Key West Fla, resided there from 1887 to 1892 and I was acting as Sub Agent at the time for W.P. Canady ___? of Washington D.C.

I knew Stephen Barrett well but have had no communication from him since I left Key West.

Q. Where did Stephen Barrett live the last you knew of him.

A. He lived on one of the Island Keys of Monroe Co Fla. I think Key L__? not far from (Chuckalusky[5]) Fla. Mail would reach him either at Key West or (Chuckalusky) if he still resides at those places. But it now occurs to my mind that sometime in 1892, a difficulty occurred on one of the Keys, in the neighborhood of where Barrett lived growing out of the attempt to arrest a man by Caleb Roton? and M__? Thompson, deputy sheriffs of Monroe Co Fla, and it is possible _____ and I rather think Barrett was in some way connected with that difficulty and had to leave the neighborhood. The difficulty I speak of these (deputys) killed a man in attempting to arrest him, I do not remember the (mans) name who was killed but think the man was killed was charged with the (raping) his own daughter.

Q. Did you know Andrew Anderson?

A. Yes sir, but I do not know where he is.

Q. Did you know Samuel J. Walters Jr.?

A. Yes sir, very well, he is a colored man and is at present principal of the Monroe Colored School at Key West Fla. If I remember rightly Stephen (Barretts) wife was a white woman or very nearly white, he and his wife were in my office when his declaration was made at set. I had formerly been County Judge of Monroe Co. Samuel

---

[5] Chokoloskee, Florida

J. Walters Jr. would probably know where Barrett is.

Questions understood and answers are correctly recorded in this deposition.

>James Dean
>Deponent.

Sworn to and subscribed before me this 18 day of Feb 1896, and I certify that the contents were fully made known to deponent before signing.

>CM Gilpin
>Special Examiner.

Richard Hamilton's Whereabouts

February 26, 1896 Key West

J. A. Davis, Esqr.
Special Examiner
U. S. Pension Bureau

Dear Sir

I regret very much not being able to see you when in Key West. Since your departure Steven (sic) Barrett has been to see me and requested me to write you and inform you of his whereabouts. He is living on one of the Bay Keys known as the Ten Thousand Islands and is the man whose application was made out by James Dean and was examined by _____ of the city he is originally from New Orleans if you should at any time desire to see him you can let me know and I will endeavor to have him here at the appointed time to (meet?) you. Be kind enough to let me know a little in advance, as it would be necessary for me to write to him. I believe he is the man you were making enquiry for when at Key West.

                Very Respectfully
                        N. F. English

Claimant located

March 2, 1896 Jacksonville, Fla.

Department of Interior,
Bureau of Pensions.

Hon. Commissioner of Pensions
Washington, D. C.

Sir:

Relating to case No 996.404 of Stephen Barrett and which was returned without report the 5th ___, with a suggestion that the case be returned to an Examiner __ Newberne, N.C. for the purpose of locality said Barrett. I have then chosen to report that I have located said Stephen Barrett at Ten Thousand Islands. This information is from reliable parties at Key West, Fla, and I am further informed that said is from New Orleans, La. and ___ to __ papers will show that there is another claim (__ with the Barrett papers) made by a woman at New Orleans alleging she is the widow of said Stephen Barrett.

I respectfully request that the papers be returned to me for investigation.

Very respectfully
Your Obt. Svt. JA Davis

DEPOSITION A
Nelson F. English

October 7, 1896 Key West

Case of Stephen Barrett alias Richard Hamilton, No. 996.404

On this seventh day of Oct, 1896, at Key West, County of Monroe State of Florida, before me, J. A. Davis, a Special Examiner of the Pension Office, personally appeared Nelson F. English, who, being by me first duly sworn to answer truly all interrogatories propounded to him during this Special Examination of aforesaid pension claim, deposes and says:

I am 48 yrs of age. No occupation at present, was formerly postmaster under President Arthur and served four years and have served sixteen years besides, as Dep. Post Master and also have been in the Custom House service for three years. Key West is my home and I have lived here since a small boy. I know Stephen Barrett as Richard Hamilton. The first I knew him as Stephen Barrett was after you had been here. He came to my place of business and I asked him if he had been in the U.S. service and he said yes he served in a La. Regt., under the name Stephen Barrett for three years and that he was applying for a pension, that James Dean made out his application for him and that he was examined by Dr. Livingston.

I have known Richard Hamilton some six, or seven years, or it may be longer. He has lived on the Thousand Islands ever since I have known him until recently he has moved to Cape Sable. He is an alligator and Plume Bird Hunter and raises produce and burn? charcoal and he brings them here and ships them. I think he is a married man, because when he was at my place he had his little boy with him. I never saw his wife.

I never had any conversation with him in regard to his history, or life in New Orleans. I do not know when he left there. I never knew him to live in this City. It was reported here that he is married to a white woman and for that reason he cannot live here.

He is an Indian looking man, tall, raw boned. I should judge he is over six feet tall, his complexion is Copper color like an Indians, black and nearly straight hair, he looks like a "Creole French like some of those Louisianans" he wears a mustache and I judge him to be about fifty five years old.

I have never noticed any peculiarity about his walk, he appears to be a straight well built man. After you were here last spring I saw Hamilton here and then I wrote to you as to his whereabouts and that when you expected to return here I would let him know. I received a letter from you a little over a month ago, or about that time and immediately after I wrote to him and since then I have again sent a verbal message that you would be here. There is no post office where he lives and I had to watch my chance and send by a boat going over there. I have not heard from him since I sent the message to him. His occupation takes him away from his home and he may not have received my message.

I have fully understood all your questions.

I think Andrew Anderson lives over where Hamilton lives. There is no such man in Key West, where I know and the man I refer to I only knew as Andrew, but I think he must be Andrew Anderson.

My answers have been correctly recorded.

        N. F. English
            Deponent.

Sworn to and subscribed before me this 7th day of October 1896, and I certify that the contents were fully made known to deponent before signing.

        JA Davis
            Special Examiner.

DEPOSITION B
Joseph Pinkney

October 7, 1896 Key West

Deposition B case of Stephen Barrett, alias Richard Hamilton, No. 996.464

On this seventh day of Oct 1896, at Key West, County of Monroe, State of Florida, before me, J. A. Davis, a Special Examiner of the Pension Office, personally appeared Joe Pinkney, who, being by me first duly sworn to answer truly all interrogatories propounded to him during this Special Examination of aforesaid pension claim, deposed and says:

I am 50 years of age. A ___ and ___ by occupation. My post office address is Key West, Fla. I never knew Stephen Barrett by that name until he told me. I came to Key West the fall of 1871. In about 1886 I went and became acquainted with Richard Hamilton. He has not lived here since I have lived here. I heard that he did live here before I came here and used to drive a Dray.

I remember meeting you here last spring in Feb, or March and your inquiring for Stephen Barrett. I did not know Stephen Barrett by that name when you were here, but after you had gone from here I saw Richard Hamilton and asked him what was his name when he was a soldier and he told me Stephen Barrett. I was over on the

Thousand Islands hunting once and he told me that he had lived in Savannah. I did not ask him and he did not tell me what Regt he was in during the war.

Ever since I have known him he has lived in the Thousand Islands, but since you were here he told me he was going to move to Cape Sable. His occupation is Alligator and Bird Plume hunting and Building Boats and a little farming and a coal burner. He is frequently off hunting and it would be difficult for a stranger to find him. He is married to a 'Cracker' woman, a white woman. He has been married ever since I have known him. I have heard him say he lived in New Orleans. He never told me any particulars of his life there.

___ came over to ask him about his name, he told me he had been a soldier. After you had gone from here and when I met him I thought of your enquiries and asked him and then he told me his name was Stephen Barrett. I asked him then if he was an applicant for a pension and he said he was and then I told him he must be the man you were looking for.

He is very tall, I judge six feet or over, a raw-boned man. He is a copper colored man, looks like he might have Indian blood in him and his hair is black and pretty straight and he wears a heavy mustache. He has a little curious walk, he is not a crippled man, but he has some defect in his walk. He is a little bow-legged. I judge him to be a man between 55 and 60. He may not be that old, he is pretty active, he does not look to be a helpless man by any means.

I do not know Andrew Anderson. The way I came to know Hamilton so well I used to order his goods, or small stores from New Orleans for him. I ordered goods from New Orleans on my own responsibility, it was from a house that I dealt with and was not suggested by Hamilton. I have not seen Hamilton (or Barrett as he claims to be) since last spring. I have no interest in this matter. I have fully understood all your questions. My answers have been correctly recorded.

     Joseph Pinkney

Sworn to and subscribed before me this 7th day of October 1896, and I certify that the contents were fully made known to deponent before signing.

     J A Davis
     Special Examiner

ACT OF JUNE 27, 1890.

DECLARATION FOR WIDOW'S PENSION.

To be executed before a Notary Public, Justice of the Peace, or any officer competent to administer oaths who has a seal.

State of Louisiana, County of St Charles, SS.

On this 11th day of November, A. D. one thousand eight hundred and ninety six, personally appeared before me, a clerk of court within and for the County and State aforesaid, Sarah Barrett, aged (blank) yeas, a resident of the (blank) of Hahnsville P.O. County of St Charles, and State of Louisiana, who, being duly sworn according to law, declares that she is the widow of Stephen Barrett, who enlisted under the name of Stephen Barrett at (blank), on the 20 day of August, A.D. 1863 in Co. C – 99th regt. and served at least ninety days in the late War of the Rebellion, who was HONORABLY DISCHARGED on the 23 day of April, 1866 and who died (blank), 1886.

That she was married under the name of Sarah Miller, to said Stephen Barrett, on the (blank) day of (blank) 18(blank), by their master, at before the war – there being no legal barrier to said marriage. _____ was married previously to marrying the said Stephen Barrett. That she has not remarried since the death of the said Stephen Barrett. That she is without other means of support than her own daily labor. That the names and dates of births of all the children of the soldier now living and who are under sixteen years of age are as follow:

No children.

That she has never heretofore applied for pension. The number of such former application is _____.

That she makes this declaration for the purpose of being placed on the pension roll of the United States, under the provisions of the Act of June 27, 1890.

She hereby appoints, with full power of substitution and revocation, B___ Roberts, (blank) of Washington, D. C. her true and lawful attorney to prosecute her claim, the fee to be TEN DOLLARS as prescribed by law.

That her POST-OFFICE ADDRESS is Hahnsville, County of St Charles, State of Louisiana.

	her
W H Fisher)	Sarah X Barrett
Zeno Jupter	mark
Two witnesses who write sign here	

The Act of June 27, 1890, *requires*, in a widow's case:

1. That the soldier served at least NINETY DAYS in the War of the Rebellion and was HONORABLY BISCHARGED.
2. Proof of soldier's death. Death cause need not have been due to Army service.
3. That widow is "without other means of support than her daily labor."
4. That widow was married to solider prior to June 27, 1890, the date of the act.
5. That all pensions under this Act commence from date of receipt of application in Pension Bureau.

Also personally appeared William Martin, residing at St Charles Parish, and Nelson Whitehead residing at St Charles Parish, persons whom I certify to be respectable and entitle to credit, and who, being by me duly sworn, say that they were present and saw Sarah Barrett, the claimant, sign her name or make her mark to the foregoing declaration that they have every reason to believe from the appearance of said claimant and their acquaintance represents for herself to be, and that they have interest in the prosecution of this claim.

W H Fisher
Zeno Jupter
_{Two witnesses who write sign here}

his
William X Martin
mark

his
Nelson X Whitehead
Mark

AFFIDAVIT
William Martin & Nelson Whitehead

December 14, 1896 St. Charles, Louisiana

GENERAL AFFIDAVIT

In the matter of Sarah Barrett widow of Stephen . Widow No 531,374, Co C. 99th

On this 14 day of December, A. D. 1896 personally appeared before me, Clerk of Court, within and for the County and State aforesaid, duly authorized to administer oaths, William Martin & Nelson Whitehead, aged 80 & 60 years, residents of _____, in the County of St Charles, and State of Louisiana, whose Post Office address is Hahnville, well known to me to be reputable and entitled to credit, and who being duly sworn, declared in relation to the aforesaid case as follows:

That they knew Stephen Barrett, that he died in the year 1886, that Stephen Barrett & Sarah Barrett were married by their former master, Col. Whitehead before the war, that they saw them married and since that time have known the two to live together as man and wife until the death of the husband.

That this affidavit was written by the clerk of court on the 14 day of December 1896 in their presence from their oral statement and that they were not aided or prompted by a person or written document.

Further declared that they have no interest in said case and are not concerned in its prosecution.[6]

    William Martin (his mark)

    Nelson Whitehead (his mark)

Witnesses:
  H. S. Cox
  A. Madere

---

[6] Another affidavit for William Martin & Nelson Whitehead was written a month later, on January 4, 1897. It says the same as this 1896 affidavit but includes the date of Stephen Barrett's death - March 4, 1886. Affidavit of February 11, 1897 adds that Sarah and Barrett were never divorced to their (Martin & Nelson) knowledge.

Affidavit
William Martin & Nelson Whitehead

February 23, 1897 St. Charles Co. Louisiana

GENERAL AFFIDAVIT

In the matter of Sarah Barrett - Widow of Stephen Barrett

On this 23 day of February A.D. 1897, personally appeared before me, a clerk of court, within and for the County and State aforesaid, duly authorized to administer oaths, William Martin & Nelson Whitehead, aged 80 and 60 years, a resident of St. Charles, in the county of St. Charles, and State of Louisiana, whose Post Office address is Hahnville.

_____, well known to me to be reputable and entitled to credit, and who being duly sworn, declared in relation to the aforesaid case as follows:

That they were acquainted with Stephen Barrett and that he never was in the military or naval service of the United States prior to August 1863, nor since April 1866 - he having lived with us on same plantation before and after he went in the army. That his widow Sarah Barrett has no property and other means of support except her manual labor, which facts they know of their own knowledge being close neighbors to her.

That this affidavit was written by the clerk of the court in their presence from their oral statement made to the ___ at the Court House on the 23rd February 1897 and that they were not aided or prompted by any person or written document.

They further declared that they have no interest in said case and are not concerned in its prosecution.

    William Martin (his mark)
    Nelson Whitehead (his mark)

WITNESSES:
  A. Madere

Affidavit
Isam Anthony & Paul Cooper

March 11, 1897 Kalona, St. Charles Co., Louisiana

Affidavit that the Claimant has Remarried, and that She is without means of Support than her Daily Labor.

Act of June 27, 1890.

    I, Isam Anthony and Paul Cooper of the town of Kalona, County of St. Charles, and State of Louisiana, do solemnly swear that we are neighbors of Sarah Barrett who is the Widow of Stephen Barrett, deceased, on whose account she applies for pension under the provisions of the act of June 27, 1890, and that for the past Twenty to Thirty years we have been well acquainted with the said Sarah Barrett; that from our frequent intercourse and conversations, and from other circumstances, we have every reason to believe, and we do believe, that the said Sarah Barrett has not remarried since the death of the above-mentioned Stephen Barrett. Further, we say that if she had remarried we have reason to believe that we should have known it.

We also believe from the knowledge we have of said widow that she neither owns nor has in use any property of any kind from which a revenue can be derived; that she has no income or present means of support than her daily labor. She has no person living legally bound for her support.

That Stephen Barrett died on Waterford Plantation, St. Charles Parish in the State of Louisiana in the month of March 1886 and was buried there; we were present and attended his funeral. We further certify that Sarah Barrett married Stephen Barrett in the year 1880 by Rev. Louis Ruffin in St. Charles Parish, and we were witnesses to the ceremony, and further that they were not previously married prior to their marriage in the year 1880. Further that Sarah Barrett has no means of support and depends upon friendly assistance for her support. We testify to the above facts from personal knowledge, and further that we have no interest in the prosecution of this claim.

     Isam Anthony
     Paul Cooper

ATTEST:
Henry Ballou
Edward Vaucresson

Barrett alias Hamilton

March 31, 1897 Jacksonville, Fla.

Special Examination Division Jacksonville
Department of the Interior
Bureau of Pensions

Hon. Commissioner of Pensions,
Washington, D.C.

Sir:

Having this month received some additional ___ in case No. 531.374 Sarah Barrett alleged Widow of Stephen Barrett, late of Co. G. 99th U.S.C.T. I desire to submit an explanation for the apparent delay in sending my report. In connection with the above cited claim there is a claim, N. 996.404, Stephen Barrett, alleging he's the identical person who performed the service under the name of Steven Barrett in Co. G. 99th U.S.C.T. The address of the alleged widow is ___ St Charles Parish, La. and that of alleged soldier is given as Key West, Monroe County, Florida. The papers were originally received in this ___ ___ and were returned without report February 5th, '96, "claimant not found." Subsequently, I am informed that Special Examiner ___ made a search for said Steven Barrett and failed to locate him. March 20 '96 the papers again came into my hands and another search by myself failed to locate the alleged soldier. After considerable correspondence, I was informed that said Barrett lived on one of the Thousand Islands. After that information was received, I was again at Key West on other ___ and learned that he had changed his abiding place ___ Cape Sable, Florida. While at Key West, I obtained some ___ ___ to the claim but was unable to see the claimant. The failure Mr _____ and ___ to locate said Barrett was due to the fact he is not known by that name he is known as John Hamilton. Barrett alias Hamilton ___ a midwife, hunts and fishes and occasionally visits Key West.

Cape Sable is in the extreme point of the Peninsula and there is no post office and no regular transportation. ___ trip to_____Fla., it was my intention to go to Cape Sable, but the charge for a suitable boat, at this season of the year, I found would be twelve dollars per day (not including meals) and the trip might_____. I felt some hesitation about incurring so much expense, as I can probably obtain transportation later in the season at greatly reduced prices. _____ advised to the contrary I will make the last ___ ___ possible and attend to the matter later in the season. Trusting my action will meet with your approval.

Very respectfully

Your Obd. Svt.
J. A. Davis
Special Examiner

PS Perhaps I should state that although the above decided case came from the Law Div., prosecution was barred by the statute of limitations before the papers reached my hands.

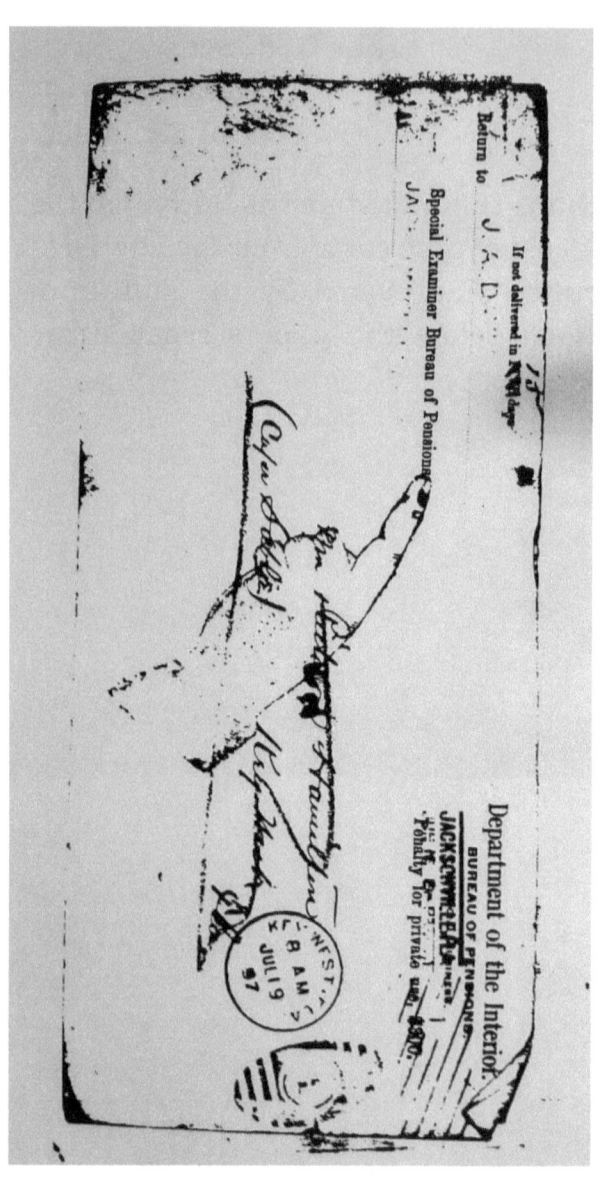

July 1897

Claim of *Sarah Barrett*
widow of *Stephen "*

Co. *C.* 99th Reg't *U.S.C.I.* Vols

No. *531,374*

WASHINGTON, D. C., *Aug 2,* 189*7.*

Hon. Commissioner of Pensions:

SIR—We have the honor to call your special attention to the above entitled case. Please advise us promptly of its status, and if any evidence is required, please so inform us.

General Law.

In the above cited claim filed Nov 28, '96 the last evidence in which was filed June 6-1897. Information is respectfully asked as to whether the claim has been placed in the Special Examiner's Division.

Yours respectfully, SUCCESSOR
WILLIAM FITCH & CO.,
Attorneys.

Peculiar, Lawless, Desperate Character

August 30, 1897 Jacksonville, Fla.

Hon Commissioner of Pensions
    Washington, D. C.

Sir:

I have the honor to return, herewith, all the papers in case No. 996.404, of Stephen Barrett, late of Co., G 99th U.S.C. Inf., address given as Key West, Fla together with papers in case. No. 531.374, of Sarah Barrett, alleged widow of Stephen Barrett, where post address is, Killona, St. Charles Parish.

The above described claims have been consolidated and were referred to this Dist. for examination at Key West, Fla. to determine whether the Stephen Barrett ___ referred to is the same person who performed in services alleged. These papers have been in the hands of other examiners who failed to locate the claimant and my first efforts were with ___ ___.

Since then, by correspondence and numerous inquiries, aided by others, I have learned that a man known as Richard Hamilton is the person who filed the claim under the name of Stephen Barrett. This information was obtained in March 1896 and on my ___ visit to Key West (Oct 1896). I took the testimony of two persons who testify to the alias, but I failed to locate the claimant. I have tried to reach him by letter through the mails and have corresponded with my ___ informant (Mr. Nelson English) but did not receive a reply.

Richard Hamilton is peculiar and a lawless, desperate character and difficult to get at. He is living with a white woman and also a forger. He, for these reasons cannot come to Key West (except in the night.) At one time I was informed he lived on one of the Ten Thousand Islands, subsequently at Cape Sable and at present his whereabouts is somewhere in the swamps and thickets, as a short time ago the officers of the law who were sent to arrest him were driven off at the point of a ___ Rifle and Barrett alias Hamilton took to the thicket. There is no regular mode of conveyance to the Ten Thousand Islands, or to Cape Sable and I can only reach said places by chartering a sail boat or Launch at a cost of not less than $7.00 per day and it will require at least six days, possibly ten days to make the trip. Last winter the expenses were $12.00 per day and I decided to postpone the matter until the ___ season was over. I started with this trip with the intention of going to Cape Sable and engaged a boat for $7.00 per day, but the owner backed out at the last moment because it is about the hurricane season and he was afraid to return.

I am quite confident I can find said Barrett alias Hamilton, but in view of the

expenses in time and money I have thought best to report the situation and await further instructions. The widow's claim does not enter into the matter as by her own admission before Special Examiner Montgomery she has no ___ ___
Prosecution in her case, as well the case of Stephen Barrett was barred by the State of Louisiana, where the papers were ___ but the alleged widow has continued to file affidavits and two of the affidavits at least, (Wm Martin and Nelson Whitehead) of the execution of their affidavits can be established should be prosecuted for aiding in a false claim and for perjury.

I do not see that any conclusion can be reached in the Stephen Barrett case until he has been interviewed and if it is the decision of the Bureau that (regardless of time and expenses) his testimony be secured I will promptly obey such instructions.

        Very respectfully
        Your Obd., Svt.,
        J. A. Davis
        Special Examiner

8.

(B-146, x)
ACT OF JUNE 27, 1890.

INVALID PENSION. #996404

Claimant: Richard Hamilton als Stephen Barrett
P.O.: Key West   Rank: Pvt
County: Monroe   Company: G & C
State: Fla   Regiment: 99 U.S. C'd H'y Inf

Rate: $ _____ per month, commencing _____

Disabled by _____   REJECTED

RECOGNIZED ATTORNEY.

Name: E.S. Kurtz   Fee, $ ____   Agent to pay.
P.O.: City   Articles filed _____, 189__

APPROVALS.

Submitted for Reje- Nov 14, 1897. Sayre V.E. Examiner.

Approved for
Rejection on the ground that it is not shown that Richard Hamilton rendered the service in Co. G of 99th reg't under the name of Stephen Barrett although given the benefit of a[n] examination.

M.G. Robertson Legal Reviewer
Nov 16, 1897

Not now pensioned under other laws. Last paid to _____, 18___, at $ ____
Pensioned from _____, 18___, at $ _____ for _____

SERVICE SHOWN BY RECORD.

Enlisted Aug 20, 1863 and honorably discharged April 2d, 1866
Re-enlisted ____ 18__   honorably discharged ____ 18__
Declaration filed Jany 27, 1891, alleges permanent disability, not due to vicious habits,
from rupture

C147

Letter of Rejected Claim to Richard Hamilton

December 8, 1897 Key West

DEPARTMENT OF THE INTERIOR.
BUREAU OF PENSIONS.
WASHINGTON, D. C.

No. 996.404 Richard Hamilton alias Stephen Barrett, Co. C 99 Reg't U S C Vol Inf

Sir:

Your above entitled claim for pension filed under the Act of June 27, 1890 was rejected Nov 26 1897 under the ground that it is not shown that you rendered service in Co "C" 99 Regt U. S. C. ___ under the name of ___ Stephen Barrett although you were given the benefit of a special examination.

Very respectfully

_____[7]

Commissioner

Richard Hamilton
Key West Fla.

---

[7] Name is illegible

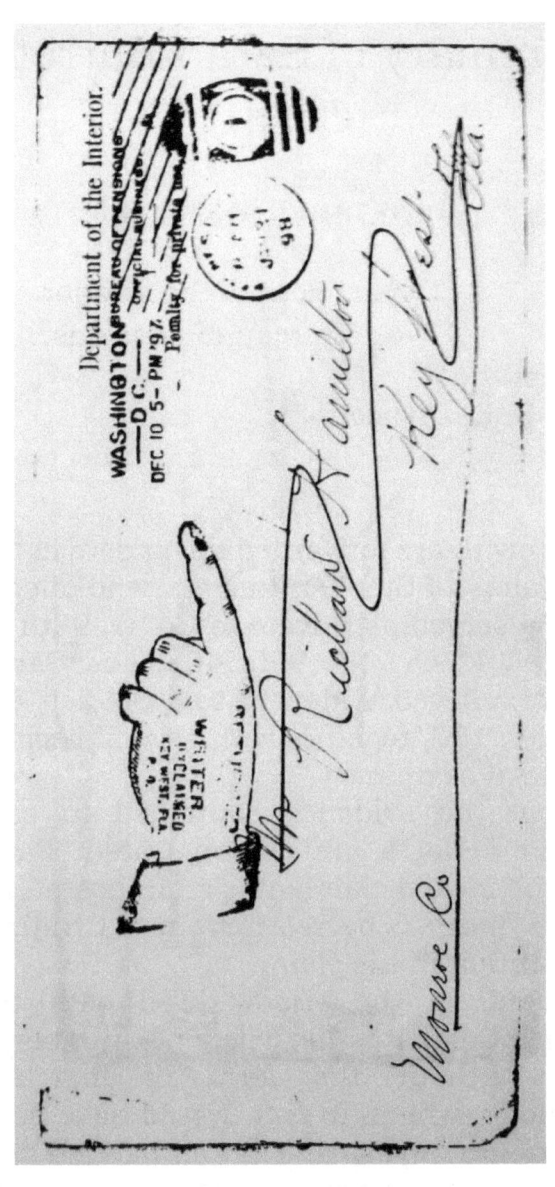

January 31, 1898

Summary of Sarah Barrett Case

February 11th, 1898 Washington, DC

Department of the interior,
Bureau of Pensions,

Chief of the
S. E. Division.

Sir:

Herewith are forwarded the papers in the two claims of Stephen Barrett, who alleges that he served as private in Co. G, 98th U. S. C. V. I., Or. No. 996, 408, and Sarah Barrett, alleged Widow of said Soldier, Or. No. 531, 137, together with several reports of special examiners.

From the evidence contained in said reports to facts are demonstrated: First; stop the invalid claimant is an imposter. All papers are barred from Criminal prosecution in his claim.

Second: . The Widow lived with the genuine Soldier as his wife for a number of years without the form of marriage ceremony, which, in fact, would have been invalid, anyway, as she has a husband now living, from whom she has never been divorced.

The Widow filed a declaration November 6th, 1891, which developed the foregoing socks as to her relations with the soldier.

Prosecution upon that paper is barred. On December 3, 1896, however another Declaration was filed by one Sarah Barrett, signed by Mark in the presence of w. H. Fisher, and Zeno (Jupter), together with William Martin and Nelson Whitehead as identifying Witnesses, such paper being executed before J. B. Martin, Clerk of the Court. The claimant and all of the Witnesses are residents of St-Charles Parish, in or near Hahnville, La. In this declaration the Widow alleges that she was married to Steven (sic) Barrett, lived with him during his life and until his death, and is his lawful Widow; that she was never married prior to her marriage to said soldier, Steven Barrett; that when she married him her name was Sarah Miller, and that said marriage was performed by their master before the war.

In an affidavit filed in this claim, executed December 14th, 1896, William Martin and Nelson Whitehead testified that they " new well Steven Barrett the soldier; that he died in the year 1886; that Steven Barrett and Sarah Barrett were married by their former master Colonel Whitehead before the war; thought they saw them married; and since that marriage have known the two to live together as husband and wife until the death of the soldier."

Affiants signed by Mark in the presence of M. S. Cox and A. Maden, said paper being executed before J. B. Martin, Clerk of the Court. Affiants and witnesses reside in

Hahnville, La. The same affiants in affidavit of January 4th, 1897, in the presence of Adam Darensburg and Alfred Willis, all of Hahnville, La., and executed before J. B. Martin, Clerk of the Court, testified that said marriage occurred before the war.

Same parties, in another affidavit executed January 23rd, 1897, in presence of A. Robbins & J. K. Alexander, of Hahnville, La., and executed before J. B. Martin, Clerk of the Court testified that " they were acquainted with Sara (sic) Barrett before her marriage with Stephen Barrett; that she had not been married before she married him, and that she has not remarried since the death of said; have known Sarah Barrett since the war, and have ever since lived close to one another."

Isam Reed and Nelson Whitehead, in affidavit executed February 4th, 1897, and presence of F. Loud and Charles Washington, and executed before J. B. Martin, Clerk of the Court, state that " they knew Steven Barrett before he was married to Sarah Barrett; thought he was never married before he married her; that they were never divorced, and that she has not remarried since his death; that they know these facts of their own knowledge, having been acquainted with them both before they were married, and have lived near neighbors ever since." These parties likewise live in Hahnville, La.

Sarah Barrett, claimant in the Declaration filed in 1891, States, in deposition of July 18th, 1895, before special examiner J. W. Montgomery, that she lives in Kelona, St Charles Parish, La.; that she claims pension as the Widow of Steven Barrett, the soldier of aforesaid service; that she was married to one Sam Miller during the war; married him by license from the St Charles Courthouse; (exhibiting to the examiner the marriage certificate signed by B. Boggs, Provost Marshal, dated December 5, 1864) that she lived with said Sam Miller for 13 years of his wife, when he deserted her and took up with another woman; that she waited 1 year and 6 months after said desertion by her husband, Sam Miller, when she took up with Stephen Barrett, the soldier, and that they live together for nine years, when he died; that she was never divorced from her husband Sam Miller, and that he is now living in St John Parish, La.; that she was never regularly married to Steven Barrett, the soldier; they had no license and no preacher; that Steven Barrett, the soldier, never had any other name than Stephen Barrett; that he came to that locality from Virginia with his master, Colonel Peter Whitehead.

In all salient points, the evidence given by the climate in this deposition is supported by. In the deposition of one Isom Anthony, of Kelona, La.; in his deposition of same date before special Examiner.

In view of the foregoing facts, it is believed there can be no doubt that the claimant, Sarah Barrett, in the Declaration filed in 1891, and the climate, Sarah Barrett, in the Declaration filed in 1896, are one in the same person.

Therefore, it is requested that these papers be placed in the hands of a special examiner familiar with criminal work, whose District in braces St. Charles Parish, La., with instructions to proceed there, and ascertain first, if, in point of fact, said parties are not one in the same person; he said then secure the statement of the officer before whom all the papers were executed --J. B. Martin, Clerk of the Court-- in which it should please set forth whether the names were signed before him, as they prefer to have been, and whether the Oaths were administered by him. likewise the depositions of the witnesses to the signatures of the claimant--- William Martin, Nelson Whitehead, Isom Reed--- that their names were signed by them in the oath subscribed to buy them. The special examiner should Endeavor to secure the hearinbefore mentioned marriage certificate of the marriage of Samuel Miller to the claimant, which should appear as an exhibit in his report. The papers should then be placed in the hands of a special examiner his territory and braces St John's parish, La., with instructions to locate the suds Sam Miller, who, it is alleged, it's still living, and secure from him a deposition showing whether he was married to the climate and weather any divorce was ever secured by either party.

This letter should be made an exhibit of the examiner's report.
                Very respectfully,
                    S. A. Cuddy
                    Chief of Law Division.

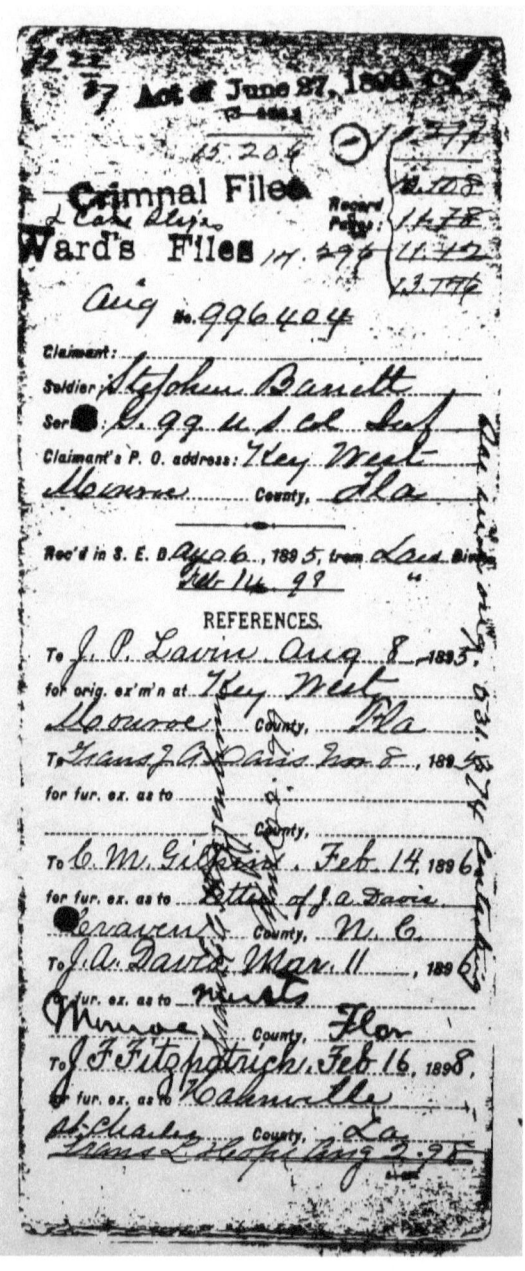

DEPOSITION B
Nelson Whitehead

May 18, 1899 Rich Bend, Louisiana

Case of Sarah Barrett, No. 531,374

On this 18th day of May, 1899 at Rich Bend, County of St. Charles State of La., before me E. C. Wigginhorn, a special examiner of the Bureau of Pensions, personally appeared Nelson Whitehead, who, being by me first duly sworn to answer truly all interrogatories propounded to him during this special examination of aforesaid claim for pension, deposes and says:

I am about ___ years of age; my post office address is Hahnville, La., occupation laborer.

I know Sarah Barrett, the claimant in this case. I lived on Col. Whitehead's (plantation) before the war and when I came back from the war I went back to Col. Whitehead's plantation. Sarah Barrett, the claimant in this case, was not living on that (plantation) before the war but I found her there when I got back after the war. I lived on Col. Whitehead's plantation about ten years after the war and (then) I went to the "Star" place which is between here and Col. Whiteheads plantation and stayed one year and then I moved into this place where I have lived ever since. Col. Whiteheads (plantation) is about two and one half miles from here. I went with Sarah Barrett, the claimant in this case, when she went before the Clerk of the Court and put in her application for pension. I guess that was three or four years (ago). Milton Cox could tell you all about it. He was looking after the case. Everybody who wants a pension gets it right from him. Whenever ___? gets a notice from Washington they get it right from him. The man who was with me and who touched the pen with me when we signed claimant's application is named William Martin, he is dead.

I think I made three affidavits for the claimant. I don't remember exactly how many as I am getting so old and it is hard to keep it all in my head. Cox would know, though. William Martin who is now dead always signed the affidavits with me. He swore to the same things that I did.

Q. Did you ever sign a joint affidavit with Isham Reed

A. Yes, sir.

Yes, I remember the time I went before the Clerk of the Court with Isham Reed and touched the pen and swore to that affidavit.

Q. What did you and William Martin swear to in the affidavits that you made in this case?

A. We swore that old man Stephen Barrett was the only husband the claimant ever had in their days.

Q. Did you not swear that Stephen Barrett was the only husband she ever had at any time?

A. I swore that he was the only husband she ever had since I have been acquainted with her.

Q. Were you sworn to every paper that you signed before the Clerk of the Court?

A. Yes, sir. The Clerk always made me hold up my right hand and be sworn and then he made me touch the pen.

Q. Here is an affidavit that purports to have been signed by you by mark and which reads as follows "that they knew Stephen Barrett, that he died in the year 1886, that Stephen Barrett and Sarah Barrett, were married by their former master Col. Whitehead before the war that they saw them married, and since that (time) have known the two to live together as man and wife until the death of the husband." In this affidavit I have omitted the formal part of? the same. This affidavit purports to have been signed by William Martin and yourself on the 14th day of December 1896; and purports to have been sworn to before J. B. Martin, Clerk of the Court. Did you sign and swear to this affidavit?

A. Yes, sir, I did.

Q. In another affidavit which reports to have been executed before J. B. Martin, Clerk of the Court, on the 4th day of January, 1897, you and William Martin are made to state as follows: "That Stephen Barrett died on the 4th day of March, 1886, but that they cannot remember the time or the date of the marriage but that Stephen Barrett was married to Sarah Barrett by their master before the war." Did you sign and swear to that affidavit?

A. Yes, sir.

Q. In another affidavit which purports to have been executed before J. B. Martin, Clerk of the Court, you and William Martin appear to have made the following sworn statement: That they were acquainted with Sarah Barrett before her marriage with Stephen Barrett and that she had not been married before she married him and that she has not remarried since the death of said Stephen Barrett, which facts they know of their own knowledge having known Sarah Barrett since before the war and have ever since lived close to one another." Did you sign and swear to that affidavit?

A. Yes, sir.

Nelson (+ his mark) Whitehead, Deponent.

Attest:
A. Labiche

S. H. Labiche

Sworn to and subscribed before me this 18th day of May 1899, and I certify that the contents were fully made known to deponent before signing.

      E. C. Wiggenhorn
        Special Examiner.

DEPOSITION D
Milton S. Cox

May 18, 1899 Rich Bend, Louisiana

Case of Sarah Barrett, No. 531,374

On this 18th day of May, 1899 at Rich Bend, County of St. Charles State of La., before me, E. C. Wiggenhorn, a special examiner of the Bureau of Pensions, personally appeared Milton S. Cox, who, being by me first duly sworn to answer truly all interrogatories propounded to him during this special examination of a claim for pension, deposes and says:

I am 56 years of age; my post office address is Hahnsville, La occupation farmer.

I have known the claimant, Sarah Barrett, since the year 1870. I have lived in this parish since the year 1870.

Q. Did you induce the claimant to file a claim for pension?

A. No, sir. I never knew anything about her claim until she came to me about it. She told me that she was the widow of Stephen Barrett and I (went) to (Bowie) Roberts a Washington, D.C. pension (attorney) for her and he sent her a blank application for pension and I went with her before the Clerk of the Court, J. B. Martin, and was with her when she signed and swore to it. She had two witnesses. She had two witnesses, William Martin and Nelson Whitehead, who signed the declaration with her as knowing all about her. They were fellow servants or something of that kind. I remember of one time when I was present when William Martin and Nelson Whitehead executed a joint affidavit in the case, and I signed as a witness that they signed it. The affidavit marked B. J. 8 is the one. I identified my signature on the same. Yes, that affidavit was duly executed in my presence. I think I was present when the affidavits marked "9", "10" and "11" were executed. I know I was present when these papers were executed since I have heard you read them. I heard these witnesses make the statements set forth in their affidavits to the Clerk of the Court and they were duly sworn to these affidavits. I can testify positively to that.

Q. Did you ever know Sam Miller?

A. Yes, sir. I do not know what has become of him. When these affidavits which you have shown me were executed, the Clerk of the Court handed them to the claimant, and she handed them to me, and I put them in the post office for her. I simply directed the envelopes and stamped them. The blanks came from the claimant's attorney, Bowie Roberts, in my care.

I simply have corresponded with the claimant's attorney for her and I do her writing in her pension case when it is required.

No, I am not a sub-agent for Bowie Roberts. I do the writing for all pension (attorney) who have clients in this neighborhood where the claimant can't do the writing themselves.

Q. Did you not know that the claimant lived for years as the wife of Sam Miller before she began living with Stephen Barrett?

A. No, sir, when I came here I found her living with Stephen Barrett as his wife. I was in this Parish for two or three years before I became acquainted with her. Yes, I know that the claimant is know ? to-day as Sarah Miller, but some call her Sarah Barrett. I have heard her called Sarah Miller, I don't deny that.

Q. Did you not know at the time that you were (attesting?) to this business for the claimant that she had lived for years as the wife of Sam Miller and that as a matter of fact she had been actually married to him?

A. No, sir, I don't know anything about that. I never gave any attention to the nickname of Sarah Miller.

Q. When you heard the claimant called Sarah Miller did not that arouse your suspicions?

A. No, sir.

The claimant has not paid me anything. None of them pays me anything unless they get their money and then they recompense me. She paid her postage fees, fifty cents, but that was sent to her attorney.

Q. How much did the claimant agree to pay you, if she got her money?

A. We made no arrangements at all.

Q. How much do they usually pay you?

A. Well it is according to how much they get. Some give me ten dollars, some five and some only a dollar. I don't make any charges. I just leave it to them.

I wrote to Simon Lyon and they advised me not to make charges of any certain amounts but to leave it to the claimants to pay me a reasonable amount. I have been advised by several not to make any demands and I tell all those I do writing for that I just leave it to them and that I can't charge them anything. I have heard this deposition read and my answers have been correctly recorded.

Deponent recalled:

I have Stephen Barrett's discharge certificate which I hereby surrender to you. William Martin who was one of the claimant's witnesses gave it to me. He and Stephen Barrett were fellow servants on Col. Whitehead's plantation, and they lived together and when Barrett died these papers were all in Martin's possession. Martin had charge of a lot of Barrett's papers – they were close friends. When the claimant executed her application for pension Martin turned this over to me. The above has been read to me and is correct.

    M. S. Cox
      Deponent

Sworn to and subscribed before me this 18th day of May 1899, and I certify that the contents were fully made known to deponent before signing.

    E. C. Wiggenhorn
      Special Examiner.

DEPOSITION A
Sarah Barrett

May 18, 1899 Green Hill, Louisiana

Case of Sarah Barrett, No. 531, 374

On this 18th day of May, 1899, at Green Hill, County St. Charles, State of La, before me E.C. Wiggenhorn a special examiner of the Bureau of Pensions, personally appeared Sarah Barrett, who, being by me first duly sworn to answer truly all interrogatories propounded to her during this special examination of aforesaid claim for pension, deposes and says:

I am about 55 years of age; my post office address is Killona, La.; occupation, I wash and patch and do anything I can get to do. I am a claimant for pension as the widow of Stephen Barrett. I don't remember what company and regiment my husband Stephen Barrett was in, but I know it was the same regiment that Isom Anthony served in because he and my husband used to talk about their army service together. I have not got my husband's discharge certificate. Milton Cox has got that.

The first time that I put in for a pension I put in with a yellow woman named Mary. She told me that she was a missionary of the Governors to go around and see the soldier's widows and carry the complaint in. She asked me my husband's name and when he died and what he died with and

she put it all down, and she went away that evening and I have not seen her from that day to this day. Then in a year or two a white man, a Special Examiner, came to see me, I do not know what his name was; it was raining? when he drove up to the house where I lived at. This Special Examiner asked me a lot of questions and then it put it in his satchel and said it was all right and drove (away?) Then in about two years I went before Mr. Martin, the Clerk of the Court, and I made out an application for pension there. Milton Cox went with me. He was the one who got me to put in my application. William Martin, Nelson Whitehead, Isom Anthony and James Wilson went with me as my witness. William Martin has been dead about three months. James Wilson has moved away – I heard – and I don't know where he is now.
Q. Did you have any other witnesses?

A. I had Isom Reed. He is living over the river. I paid Isom Anthony, Nelson Whitehead and Jim Wilson fifty cents each and I gave the Clerk of the Court Mr. Joe Martin one dollar. That was all I had. I gave Milton Cox fifty cents to get stamps and envelopes.

I was first married to Sam Miller. I was married to him during the war on Whitehead old plantation about a mile from here. I was married to Sam Miller by Elder Ruffin a colored preacher of the Baptist church on the plantation. I don't know where the license was obtained. I had my marriage paper when that Special Examiner was to see me, but I have lost it since. My son came home with the smallpox and they made me get out and scattered my papers everywhere and burned them up and whitewashed the house. I never saw the marriage paper after that. That was the night the sheriff, Mr. Louis Orr____ got married.

I lived on the "Waterford", Colonel Whiteheads plantation from the time I was married until the time my son came home with the smallpox.

I lived with Sam Miller over nine years and after he died I married Stephen Barrett.

Q. You don't mean after he died, do you? You meant after he took up with another woman, don't you?

A. Yes, sir, that is right. God knows you understand it better than I do. Sam Miller died. I could not fix the date of his death, but it is since my son had the smallpox. My son John Miller of La Place, St. John the Baptist Parish, La, told me of Sam Miller's death. Mrs. Puppan Varice also told me.

I never had but one child in my life and that was John Alexander Miller. Sam Miller was his father. He (my son) works for Dr. Lisha (Mordagie) of Laplace. Sam Miller died over there about two or three miles from Dr. Lisha (Mordagie's) place. They told me that the woman he was living with his dead too. 'Cinda, Mary Marshall, Marshall

(Foster) (dead) and a lady they called Annie were present when I was married. Cinda is dead. Mary Marshall took another husband and went away – to St. Louis I heard. "Annie" died year before last.

After Miller left I stayed single on the place without any one to help support me for one year and six months. That is straight – as straight as a loom stick. I then took up with Stephen Barrett and I lived with him about ten years when he died. I was not married to Barrett by any regular ceremony. We just took up together and I lived with him as his wife until he died.

Nelson Whitehead has been knowing me ever since the war. He lived on the same place with me when I lived with Sam Miller and also when I lived with Stephen Barrett.

I show you some letters that I got from my son and one I got from Lee Morris. I've raised Lee Morris.

Sarah Barrett, by her mark, Deponent.

Sworn to and subscribed before me this 18 day of May 1899, and I certify that the contents were fully made known to deponent before signing.

E.C. Wiggenhorn

Special Examiner.

DEPOSITION A cont.
Sarah Barrett

May 18, 1899 Green Hill, Louisiana

Case of Sarah Barrett, No. 531,374

On this 18th day of May 1899,

(previous pages are missing)

... daughter. Yes, I will give you these letters if you want them.

Yes, I was sworn by Clerk of the Court Martin when I made out my application before him. I raised my right hand and touched the pen. M. S. Cox has known me ever since the war.

Q- You go by the name Sarah Miller now don't you?

A- Yes, they nearly all call me Aunt Sarah Miller but some call me Mrs. Barrett. No, I was never divorced from Sam Miller. He went off with another woman and that was divorce enough for me. I agreed to pay Milton Cox something if I lives and succeeded in my claim, but I did not agree to pay him any particular amount.

I have heard this deposition read. I have understood the questions asked and my answers have been correctly recorded.

      Sarah (her mark) Barrett Deponent.

Attest:
    A.____
(S. Labiche)

Sworn to and subscribed before me this the 18th day of May 1899, and I certify that the contents were fully made known to deponent before signing.

                E. C. Wiggenhorn
                     Special Examiner

DEPOSITION C
Isham Reed

May 19, 1899 Sellers, Louisiana

Case of Sarah Barrett, No. 531,374

On this 19th date of May, 1899, at Sellers, county of St. Charles State of La., before me, E. C. Wiggenhorn, a special examiner of the Bureau of Pensions, personally appeared is Isham Reed, who, being by me first duly sworn to answer truly all interrogatories propounded it to him during this special examination of aforesaid claim for pension, deposes and says:

I am about 92 years of age; my post office address is Sellers, La., occupation nothing – too old to work.

I knew the claimant, Sarah Barrett, for twenty-two years before the war. We lived on the same plantation – (Valcen Mermion's) plantation. After the war she lived on Colonel Whitehead's plantation and first one place and then another in that (neighborhood). I have lived in that neighborhood since the war until last year when I came over here.

Yes, I made an affidavit for the claimant. That was before the Clerk of the Court, Martin, died. Yes, I signed and swore to the affidavit. I think Nelson Whitehead signed the affidavit with me.

Q. What did you swear to in that affidavit?

A. I swore to who she had for a husband and (that) she did not have any husband since he (died). I swore that she had Steven Whitehead for a (husband) and that she had not had any husband (since) he died.

Q. Don't you mean Stephen Barrett?

A. Yes, sir, that's him.

Q. Did you mean to swear that she was Stephen Barrett's legal widow?

A. Yes, sir.

Q. The affidavit that purports to have been signed by you and Nelson Whitehead reads as follows: "That they knew Stephen Barrett long before he was (married) to Sarah Barrett, that he was never married (before) he married her – that they were never divorced. That they know these facts their own knowledge having been acquainted with both before they were married and have lived as neighbors since. Is that in effect what you signed and swore to?

A. Yes, sir.

Q. Who induced you to sign that affidavit?

A. The claimant asked me to be witness for her.

No, Milton Cox did not ask me to make the affidavit. Yes, I think he was present when I made the affidavit but I am not sure.

Q. You knew Sam Miller, did you not?

A. Oh, yes, sir.

Q. You knew he was the claimant's first husband did you not?

A. Yes, sir.

Q. You knew he was living at the time he made this affidavit, did you not?

A. Yes, sir, I believe he was living. I know he was living then. I think he has been dead about two years. He died up in St. John's Parish.

Q. If he was the claimant's first husband and was living at the time you made the affidavit; how could the claimant be Stephen Barretts legal widow?

A. Because the claimant and Sam Miller had parted. They parted when the war was over.

Q. You know they lived together a long time after the war, don't you?

A. No, not so very long. They had parted when I came out of the war. I stayed in the war two and one half years. I served and Co. C, 10th Hy. Art. She was never married to Sam Miller. They took up together on the plantation. I have heard you read the claimant's statement to Special Examiner J. W. (Montgomery) in which she states that she was married to Sam Miller in the year 1864 and lived with him for thirteen years afterwards and would say that I did not know of her marriage to Sam Miller and that I do not think that they lived together that long after the war. I am certain that they were parted when I came out of the army. No one paid me for my affidavit in th___

I have heard this deposition read. I have understood the questions asked and my (answers) have been correctly recorded.

Isham (+ his mark) Reed
Deponent.

Attest: Alice (Reynaud)   Peter Brown
Sworn to and subscribed before me this 19th day of May 1899, I certify that the contents were fully made known to deponent before signing.

E. C. Wiggenhorn, Special Examiner.

DEPOSITION E

John Miller

May 24, 1899 LaPlace, Saint John the Baptist, Louisiana

Deposition a case of Sarah Barrett, number 531, 374

On this 24th day of May 1899 at LaPlace, County of Saint John the Baptist state of La, before me, E. C. Wiggenhorn, a special examiner of the Bureau of Pensions, personally appeared John Miller, who, being by me first duly sworn to answer truly all interrogatories propounded to him during this special examination of aforesaid claim for pension, deposes and says:

I am about 34 years of age, my post office address is LaPlace, La. My occupation is laborer. My father's name was Sam Miller. My mother's name was Sarah Miller. I was born in the year 1865. I can't read or write. I don't know anything about my mother's marriage to Sam Miller except she told me she was married to him. I was a little boy when they parted. I don't remember of their living together. My father Sam Miller is dead. He died 13th day of April one year ago. He (Sam Miller) had about three wives after he left my mother. I do not know that I ever saw my mother's marriage certificate showing her marriage to Sam Miller. After I was old enough to remember, my mother and Sam Miller got together again after they had parted but did not live long together.

My mother after she and Sam Miller parted took up with Stephen Barrett. They just took up with one another. They were never married that I know of. Stephen Barrett is dead. He died of lockjaw. After Barrett she had a man named Brown that she took up with and lived with, but she did not live with him long. After Brown she lived with Alfred Adams. He stayed with her about one year. They were not married but just took up together. She had Alfred Adams before she had Brown if I am not mistaken.

She goes by the name of Sarah Miller. I ___ ___ ___ that way. When she was living with Stephen Barrett some people called her Sarah Barrett and some called her Sarah Miller. Since Barrett's death she has been called Sarah Miller. I was the only child she had by Sam Miller.

I have understood the questions asked. I have heard this deposition read and my answer has been correctly reported.

John Miller, his Mark

Attest: _____
J. J. Waddill

Sworn to and subscribed before me this 24th day of May 1899, and I certify that the contents were fully made known to depose before signing.

E. C. Wiggenhorn
    Special Examiner.

Recommend reference to Law Division

May 24, 1899 New Orleans

Hon. H. Clay Evans,
      Commissioner of Pensions,
            Washington, D.C.

Sir: -

I have the honor to return herewith all the papers in claim No. 531.574 f "Sarah Barrett", alleged widow of Stephen Barrett, late f Co. G 99th U.S.C.Vol. Inf.; also, all the papers in claim No. 995,404 of Stephen Barrett, an imposter who alleges service in the Co. and Regt. above named, and to submit the following report relative thereto:

The papers in these claims were referred to the S.E. Division and to this district at the instance of the Law Division (see Law Division letter dated Feb. 11, 1898, - Exhibit 2, this report) which advised further examination of the widow's claim with a view to the institution of criminal proceedings against certain witnesses in the claim and against the claimant herself.

The widow filed a declaration No. 6, 1891, claiming pension as the widow of Stephen Barrett. In investigating the matter of the regularity of the execution of said declaration it developed that the claimant was legally married to one Sam

Miller prior to the date of her alleged marriage to the soldier and said Sam Miller was yet living at the time said investigation was being made. It further developed that the claimant had never been divorced from the said Miller and that as a matter of fact she had never really been married to the soldier Prosecution upon that declaration was barred, but upon the 3rd day of December, 1895, another declaration was filed in the Bureau by the alleged widow, and subsequently she filed the affidavits of William Martin, Nelson Whitehead and Isham Reed in support of her false claim, which affidavits are false, misleading and fraudulent. The Law Division letter suggests that the marriage certificate, signed by the Provost Marshall, which was exhibited to Special examiner Montgomery, be obtained if possible, that the deposition of the Clerk of the Court, J. B. Martin be secured as to the proper execution of the papers and that the depositions of the witnesses to the signatures of the claimant and the affiants be taken to the same end, and also that the testimony of the claimant's legal husband be secured.

This examination has been delayed, but since the case has been in my hands (it was turned over me last month) it was taken up by me at the earliest practicable date. I presume that the delay prior to that time was due to the congested condition of the work in this district.

The marriage certificate referred to has been lost or destroyed. About two years ago the claimant's son came home to her with the smallpox. Her neighbors sent him back where he came from, and drove the claimant off the plantation, after which they fumigated her house, burning everything burnable. She claims that she lost her marriage certificate at that time. She willingly turned over to me all the papers in her possession, which were simply a few letters addressed to her as Sarah Miller.

J. B. Martin, the Clerk of the Court, died April 10, 1897.

Sam Miller died April 13, 1898.

William Martin, one of the affiants in question, is dead.

In view of the fact that the only documentary proof of said marriage has been destroyed, and of the further fact that the husband, Sam Miller is dead, I do not think the institution of criminal proceedings against the parties in question advisable. I talked with the present Clerk of the Court of St Charles parish and he told me that he had no record of marriages of that character - that is, those performed under military authority or supervision. Besides, the claimant is an ignorant, simple-minded woman who does not seem to realize that she has done anything wrong; Nelson Whitehead seems to be remarkably dense and stupid, and Isham

Reed is very old. If I could have secured sufficient evidence to warrant the prosecution of Milton S. Cox, it would have afforded me pleasure to have recommended his criminal prosecution, as I believe him to be thoroughly dishonest and unscrupulous. In view of the admissions of the claimant and witnesses, I deemed it unnecessary to take the depositions of the witnesses to their signatures.

I recommend reference to the Law Division for consideration.

Very respectfully,

      E.C. Wiggenhorn,
        Special Examiner.

_____ Law _____ Division.

Department of the Interior,
BUREAU OF PENSIONS,

Washington, D., June 7, 1899.

No. Claim, 53,374

Cert. No. _____

Claimant, Sarah Barrett

Soldier, Stephen Barrett

Co. G, 99 Reg't U.S.C.T. Inf

Respectfully referred to Chief Southern Division. The claimant has undoubtedly been guilty of filing a false claim but, in view of the death of material witnesses and the burning of the certificate of marriage, it is not believed a successful criminal prosecution could be sustained, and it is not deemed expedient to institute same. No further action is necessary by this division.

Wm K C _____ Chief of Law Division

Law Division - No further action necessary

June 7, 1899 Washington, D. C.

Department of the Interior,
BUREAU OF PENSIONS,

No. Claim, 531,374
Claimant, Sarah Barrett
Soldier, Stephen Barrett
Co. G, 99 Reg't U. S. C. V. Inf

Respectfully referred to Chief Southern Division.

The claimant has undoubtedly been guilty of filing a false claim but, in view of the death of material witnesses and the burning of the certificate of marriage, it is not believed a successful criminal prosecution could be sustained, and it is not deemed expedient to institute same.

No further action is necessary by this division.

_____[8]

Chief of Law Division

---

[8] Name illegible

CLAIM FOR BOUNTY, ARREARS OF PAY, ETC.

October 9, 1901 Key West

State of Florida, county of Monroe, SS.

On this 9th day of October 1901, personally appeared Stephen Bartlett (sic) who being duly sworn according to law, declares:

That I am the identical person who was in the military service of the United States, and whose record as such is as follows

Rank	Company	Regiment	Date of Entry Into Service.	Date of Discharge
Priv.	"G".	99 La.	1862	1865

That said soldier was never in the military or naval service of the United States except as herein stated.

And that I hereby make application for all arrears of pay, travel pay, allowances, or bounty due for said services, under any act of Congress, order, regulation or decision to my case applicable.

That I have not sold, loaned nor bartered soldier's discharge or any portion of or interest in any money due me: and I hereby authorize and empower, with full power of substitution, HARVEY SPALDING & SONS, of Washington, D. C., my attorneys to prosecute this, my claim, and to do and perform any act necessary to be done in my name in the adjudication hereof before the Departments and U. S. Courts.

My Post Office address is Everglade, Fla.

> Stephen Barrett (his mark)

Witnesses to signature:
F. W. Johnson
Geo. G. Brooks.

Also personally appeared F. W. Johnson, residing at Key West, Fla., and Geo. G. Brooks, residing at Key West, persons whom I certify to be respectable and entitled to credit, and who, being by me duly sworn, say that they were present and saw this claimant sign the foregoing application; that they have every reason to believe from the appearance of said claimant and their acquaintance, that the claimant is the identical person represented; and that they have no interest in the prosecution of this claim.

> F. W. Johnson.
> Geo. G. Brooks

Sworn to and subscribed before me this 9th day October, A. D. 1901, and I do hereby certify that the contents of the above declaration &c., were fully made known and explained to the applicant and witnesses before swearing, and that I have no interest, direct or indirect, in the prosecution of this claim.

J. M. Phipps,
    Notary Public.

Letter to J.M. Phipps

November 26, 1901 Washington, D. C.

Department of the Interior,
Bureau of Pensions,

Mr. J. M. Phipps,
Notary Public,
Key West, Monroe Co., Florida

Sir:

Referring to the claim of Stephen Barrett, alleged late private in Co. G, 99th U. S. Colored Infantry, Original No. 996,404, in connection with which a declaration was filed in this Bureau on October 14, 1901, under the provisions of the act of June 27, 1890, as amended by the act of May 9, 1900, purporting to have been executed before you on the 9th day of October, 1901, and to which F. W. Johnson and George W. Brooks, of Key West, Fla, were the identifying and attesting witnesses, I have to request that you will, with the return of this letter in the enclosed envelope which requires no postage, inform this Bureau whether the claimant, that is the person who signed said declaration before you, was sworn to the same by you, and is personally known to you, and whether his residence is in a place accessible for an officer of this Bureau to call upon him and secure a sworn statement relative to the merits of the claim, provided it be deemed expedient that such a sworn statement be obtained from him by an officer of the Bureau; and, if practicable, that you further inform the Bureau about the length of time which it would take an officer to go from Key West to Everglades, Monroe Co., Fla, the post office address given by the claimant.

This information is requested in view of the fact that in the past it has been found impossible for an officer of the Bureau to locate the claimant in question ___ a declaration which he had filed in 1891.

I thank you in advance for the information which you may give the Bureau.

            Very respectfully,
                Commissioner.

Request for names of soldiers in Co. G

December 18, 1901 Washington, D. C.

Department of the Interior,
Bureau of Pensions,

The Chief of the
Records Division,
Bureau of Pensions.

Sir:

For use in the further consideration of the claim of Stephen Barrett, alleged late private, Co. G, 99th U. S. Col. Inf., Orig. No. 996,404, it is requested that you will, with the return of this letter, furnish a list of officers and comrades who served in said organization from August 20, 1863, until April 20, 1866.

If there should be any named on your records residing in or near Key West, Florida, - in which locality the claimant appears to have resided for a number of years, - it is preferred that those names be furnished.

Very respectfully,
Chief of Law Division.

List of soldiers serving in Co. G

December 19, 1901

NAME.	RANK.	PRESENT POST-OFFICE ADDRESS.
Henry Anderson	Pvt	Tallahassee, Leon Co. Fla.
Julian Augustin		Laplace, St John the Baptist Co. La.
Walter H. Hutchinson	1st Sgt.	Bristol, Hartford Co. Conn.
Aaron Hill	"	Darrow, Ascension Co. La.
Robert Leggisso	Pvt.	Thomasville, Thomas Co. Ga.
Augustus alias Ogasse Martin		Palmetto St. Laundry Co. La.
Anderson Ross	Sgt.	Donaldsonville, Ascension Co. La.
Nelson Stevens	Pvt.	Feche and Dearmle Sts. New Orleans, La.
Charles Swan	Pvt.	1123 Dufossat St. New Orleans, La.
Reddick Wiggins	Pvt.	Port Allen. W. Baton Rouge, La.

Exhibit C.

December 18, 1901 Washington, D. C.

Department of the Interior,

Bureau of Pensions,

The Chief of the
S. E. Division.

Sir:

I herewith forward the papers in the claims of Stephen Barrett alleged late private, Co. G. 99 U. S. Col. Inf., Orig. No. 996,404, and of Sarah Barrett, who alleges that her deceased husband was the identical soldier who rendered the aforesaid service, Original No. 531,374, together with several reports of Special Examiners relative thereto.

The claim of the alleged widow was rejected June 17, 1899, on the ground that at the time of her alleged marriage to the soldier she had not secured a divorce from her former husband, Miller, who was still living.

The invalid claim of Stephen Barrett was rejected November 26, 1897, on the ground that, though aided by a special examination, the claimant was unable to show that he was the identical soldier who rendered the service.

On October 14, 1901, a new declaration was filed by the invalid claimant, in which his address is given as Everglades, Monroe Co., Florida, which is the same address given by him in his former declaration. This claim was sent to the field for special examination under Law Division letter of August 2, 1895, and the widow's claim was thoroughly investigated. Special Examiner Davis, into whose hands the papers were placed for investigation of the invalid claim, returned said papers to the Bureau with a statement that it was impossible for him to locate the claimant, Stephen Barrett; that the place where he lives is very inaccessible, requiring a sailboat trip from Key West Eight or ten miles distant; that the claimant was a fugitive from justice for violation of the Florida laws, and that he, the Special Examiner, doubted whether he could be able to secure a sworn statement from the claimant, even though he could approach his home, as the marshals and other constabulary officers of the State of Florida had frequently attempted to cause the claimant's arrest, without success.

In view of these circumstances, this Bureau addressed a letter on November 26, 1901, to J. M. Phipps, notary public, Key West, Fla., before whom the declaration purports to have been executed, asking whether the paper was executed as it purported to have been, whether he had any acquaintance with the claimant, just how long it would take an officer of this Bureau to go from Key West to the claimant's home, if it should be desired that an officer be sent there.

In a letter of the 11th instant, Mr. Phipps informs the Bureau that the declaration was executed as it purports; that he is personally acquainted with the claimant, and that it will take about four or five days for an Examiner to go over from Key West to claimant's home, Everglades, Monroe County; but that the claimant is frequent in Key West.

It is requested that these papers be forwarded to the Special Examiner whose territory embraces Monroe Co, Fla., with instructions to make a thorough investigation with a view to securing evidence which will enable the Bureau to determine whether the claimant Stephen Barrett is the identical person who rendered the service alleged. If the evidence thus secured should prove, or tend to prove, that the claimant is not the soldier who rendered the service alleged, and that he has been willfully guilty of filing a false claim, then, in addition to evidence showing this to be true, the Examiner should secure evidence showing that the claimant is the identical person who executed the declaration herewith filed October 14, 1901, before Notary Public J. M. Phipps, and filed, or caused the same to be filed, in the Bureau of Pensions.

For use in connection with the claim, inasmuch as identity as seriously questioned, a list of comrades will be found with the papers herewith.

This letter should appear as an exhibit in the report of the Special Examiner.

     Very respectfully,
     Chief of Law Division

"a very stupid and ignorant negro"

December 11, 1901 Key West

PHIPPS & BROOKS.
ATTORNEYS AND COUNSELORS AT LAW.
KEY WEST, FLORIDA

Dec. 11th, 1901.

Hon. H. Clay Evans,
    Commissioner of Pensions,
        Washington, D. C.

Dear Sir: -

In reply to your letter of the 26th., of Nov. will say that on the 9th., day of October 1901, Stephen Barrett, signed an application for a pension before me to which he was duly sworn by me, and that said applicant is personally known to me.

He claims Everglade Fla., as his post office, but I have been informed that he spends only a part of his time at that place, and the remainder of his time he is in Key West, he seems to be sort of a farmer and coal burner, on the little islands near the post office Everglade.

Everglades is about 100 miles from Key West, and can only be reached from this point by sail boat, the time consumed in making the voyage to that place would depend entirely upon the condition of the weather, it might be made in one day, and it might take four or five days.

Barrett is a very stupid and ignorant negro, and his memory as to past events is exceedingly defective, from reliable information I learned that he came to Key West, a few years after the close of the Civil War, and has been here and on the Florida Keys ever since.

                Very truly yours,
                J. M. Phipps.

Orig. No. 996.404
Stephen Barrett
Co. G, 99 Reg't U.S.C.T.
P.O.
Enlisted Aug. 20, 1863.
Discharged Apr. 20, 1866.
Disability incurred .... 18....

Department of the Interior,
BUREAU OF PENSIONS,
Washington, D.C. Dec. 19, 1901.

Chief, Army and Navy Survivors' Division:

Please furnish the names and post-office addresses of officers and comrades of Co. G, 99" Reg't U.S.C.Tr'ps.

NAME	RANK	PRESENT POST-OFFICE ADDRESS	WITNESS ACCOUNTED FOR BY—
Henry Anderson	Pvt.	Tallahassee, Leon Co. Fla.	
Julian Augustin	"	Laplace, St. John the Baptist Co. La.	
Walter H. Hutchinson	1 St.	Bristol, Hartford Co. Conn.	
Aaron Hill	"	Darrow, Ascension Co. La.	
Robert Liggins	Pvt.	Thomasville, Thomas Co. Ga.	
Augustus & Ozeme Martin	"	Plonette, St. Landry " La.	
Anderson Ross	Sgt.	Donaldsonville, Ascension Co. "	
Nelson Stearns	Pvt.	Toche & Dearnk Sts. N. Orleans "	
Charles Swan	"	1122 Dufossat St. " "	
Reddick Wiggins	"	Port Allen, W. Baton Rouge "	

There are no others on file in about organization.

Respectfully returned to Chief, ...Law........ Division, with the desired information as far as known.

................., 190....

Chief, Army and Navy Survivors' Division.

Exhibit B

December 26, 1901 Washington, D. C.

Department of the Interior,
Bureau of Pensions,

Mr. J. A. Davis,
Special Examiner,
Jacksonville, Florida.

Sir:

Find herewith the papers in the claims of Stephen Barrett, alleged service Co. G, 99th U.S.C.Inf., No. 996,404, and of Sarah Barrett, who alleges that her deceased husband was the identical soldier who served in the aforesaid company and regiment, forwarded to you for a thorough investigation to determine whether the claimant Stephen Barrett is the identical person who rendered the service alleged, as indicated in the accompanying letter of the Law Division, dated the 18th instant.

Very Respectfully,
Commissioner.

Letter to Everglades Postmaster

February 5, 1902 Jacksonville, Fla.

Department of the Interior,
Bureau of Pensions,

SIR:

Please state, on the back of this letter, whether Stephen Barrett or John Hamilton, or Richard Hamilton resides within your mail delivery, and if so, at what distance from the post-office, and in what direction. If he does not receive mail at your office, any assistance you may be able to give me in locating him, will be appreciated.

This information is desired for use in a claim for pension, No. 996,404, and it is requested that your reply, in the envelope herewith, be forwarded as soon as possible.

Very respectfully,

J. A. Davis
Special Examiner

THE POSTMASTER,
Everglades
Monroe Co. Fla.

Letter to Stephen Barrett alias Richard Hamilton

February 10, 1902 Washington, D. C.

Department of the Interior,
Bureau of Pensions,

Mr. Stephen Barrett
Everglades, Fla.

Sir:

Your letter dated January 19th left Key West, Fla. (as shown in the paperwork) February 7th and consequently, has just reached my hands this morning. At the present writing I cannot tell the exact day I will be at Everglades, but I think sometime between the 10th and 20th of next month. If you will call for your mail ___ days before, or say between the 1st and 10th of March, I will try and get a letter to you giving the exact times, or as such is possible to determine, when one has to depend on transportation via back. I wish you would inform me just how far and in which direction you reside from Everglades, as, in the ___ of our failure to meet, I could send you word, or be able to find you when I arrive at Everglades. I enclose an addressed return envelope which does not require any stamp and will appreciate an early reply.

Very respectfully,

    J A Davis
        Special Examiner.

Letter from Richard Hamilton to J A Davis

March 7, 1902 Everglade, Florida

Editor's Note: Sometimes you get a document that is just impossible to transcribe. Sadly, this one is written by Richard Hamilton (alias Stephen Barrett) but is too faded to read.

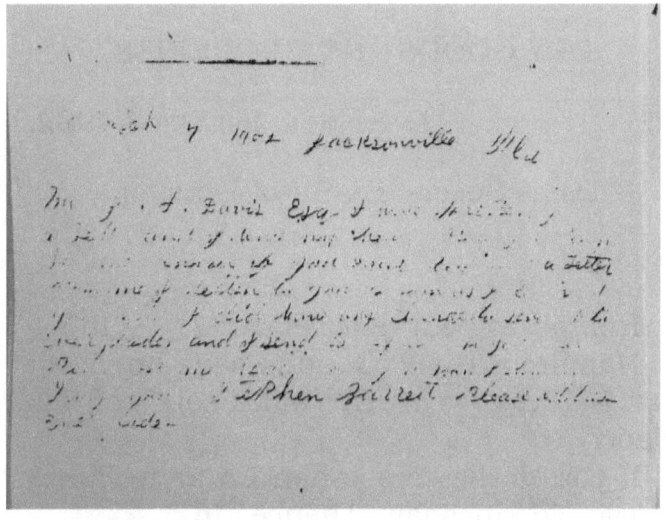

"One thing I will add that you have not asked for"

October 7, 1902 Everglade, Florida

G. H. WATSON

                        G. W. STORTER

G. H. WATSON & CO.,

DEALERS IN

DRY GOODS AND GROCERIES

                     Everglade, Fla. Oct 7 1902.

J. A. Davis Special Ex-Bu-of Pension

Fine Sir

    In reply to your letter of Oct 2 ____ to ____ J. Hamilton. His P. O. address is Key West Fla. He lives twenty five miles south of this place.

    If you desire to see him Come to Punta Gorda Wednesday Thence to _____ Thursday. Friday to Marco. Saturday to Everglade. And on to Hamiltons that evening in mail ____ that you leave Marco and it makes their trips ____ week and on Saturdays trip it don't return to Marco until Monday to connect with mail ____ leaving ____ at ____ ____ ____ Punta Rassa next ____ usually to connect with Steamer to Punta Gorda Tuesday morning.

Mail _____ could not _____ the trip any other day but Saturday and that is the only Boat with ___ ___ in this section that will be available.

One thing I will add that you have not asked for. When you have located your man ___ will find a des___ Contemptible, Lawless, Vagabond and he a negro having two living wives and two families. None of which dare to live with him for fear and violence. He attempting two lives at two different ___.

Criminal Work

Undated. Missing first pages.

Claim of Sarah Barrett No. 531374

____ married to Steven Barrett, the soldier; they had no license and no preacher. Stephen Barrett, the soldier, never had any other name than Stephen Barrett, that he came to that locality from Virginia with his master, Colonel Peter Whitehead.

The evidence given by the claimant in this deposition is supported by that in the deposition of one Isom Anthony, of Kelona, Louisiana; in his deposition of same date before said special Examiner.

In view of the foregoing facts, it is believed there can be no doubt that the claimant, Sarah Barrett, and the declaration filed in 1891, and the claimant Sarah Barrett, in the declaration filed in 1896, are one and the same person.

Therefore it is requested that these papers be placed in the hands of a special examiner familiar with criminal work, whose district embraces St. Charles Parish, Louisiana with instructions to proceed there, and ascertain first, if, in point of fact, said parties are not one in the same person; he should secure the statement of the officer before whom all the papers were executed---J. B. Martin, clerk of the court-

- and which it should please set forth whether the names were signed before him, as they purport to have been, and whether the oaths were administered by him. Likewise, the depositions of the witnesses to the signatures of the claimant--- William Martin, Nelson Whitehead, Isom Reed--- that their names were signed by them and the oath (administered by) them. The special examiner should endeavor to secure the herein before mentioned marriage certificate of the marriage of Samuel Miller to the claimant, which should appear as an exhibit in his report. The papers should then be placed in the hands of a special examiner whose territory embraces St John's Parish, Louisiana, with instructions to locate the (said) Sam Miller, who it is alleged, is still living, and secure from him a deposition showing whether he was married to the claimant and whether any divorce was ever secured by either party.

This letter should be made an exhibit of the examiner's report.

Very respectfully,

    S.A. Cuddy, Chief of Law Division

DEPOSITION D
Richard Hamilton

October 18, 1902 St Josephs Island, Fla.

Case of Stephen Barrett, No. 996.404

On this eighteenth day of October, 1902, at St Josephs Isl.,County of Monroe, State of Florida, before me, JA Davis, a special examiner of the Bureau of Pensions, personally appeared Stephen Barrett alias Richard Hamilton, who, being by me first duly sworn to answer truly all interrogatories propounded to him during this special examination of aforesaid claim for pension, deposes and says:

I am 62 years of age; my post office address is, % John A. Pitcher, Key West, Monroe Co. Fla. My occupation is _____ raising and burning (?) coal. I am a Carpenter by trade. I was born July 26th 1840, at Savannah, Ga. I was born free(?). My father was named Wm Edwards. He is dead, he died in Marion Co., Fla. There is one son living I have heard, his name is Joseph Edwards. I do not know where he lives. I go by my (mothers) name. Her name was Peggy Hamilton. Her last post office address was Elmwood, Fla. I have no brothers or sisters. Edwards owned a number of slaves. The ones that I did know, the older ones have all died. I remember one named Sophia and one named Sarah.

He did not have but one or two men (?), I do not remember them. When the Civil War broke out I was living in Marion Co. I lived in La. awhile. That was the first of 1862. I was not there very long before I went in the service. I lived at Pleasant Hill. I ran away and went out there with a half brother named John Edwards. He was white and he died out there. I enlisted right at Pleasant Hill, La. I was in Co. G. 99th Regt. U.S.C.T. I do not remember the month I enlisted. It was the last of 1862 or first of 1863. I am not sure. I was discharged the last of 1865, at Tallahassee, Fla. I never went back to La. anymore. It was about six months that I lived at Pleasant Hill, La. before I enlisted. When I enlisted I took the name Stephen Barrett. My Capt. was John Moore. He gave me that name. I never knew anybody by the name Stephen Barrett. My 1st Lieut was named (Hutchey). My 2nd Lieut was named Ferris. My orderly Sgt. first was Richardson but he got his eyes put out at Natural Bridge battle and he was succeeded by Anderson Ross. I did not have any other Ord. Sgt. (Aaron) Hill was a Sgt. but I do not remember any others. I remember one corporal named Anderson Ferris and one named John Clark and one Charley Swan and now I remember another Sgt. named (Grander), he died just before we were mustered out. From the time I enlisted the organization was called the 99th Regt. La. U.S.C.T. We were __ known as the 15th C.D.A. Inf. or as 5th La. CDA ___. I served as a private all through my service. I never was in the service before (nor) after the service. I (performed) in the 99 Regt. U.S.C.T. I was very little acquainted at La. I was not married before the war. I was not married in La. I never knew Sarah Miller. I never lived with Sarah Miller. I never knew I___ Anthony. I never knew Peter Whitehead. I do not remember the name of Wm Martin, or Nelson Whitehead, or Isham Reed, nor John Miller. I do not know them. There was a man in the 99th Regt. who was named John Miller. He did not belong to my company, I do not know what company he belonged to. My bunkmate was (Hank) Davis and Robert (Legham) (Leggins).[9] They belonged in La. I do not know whether they are living. I was given a physical examination when I enlisted. I do not remember what age I gave them. I lack one inch of being 6 feet tall now. I do not know my height when I went in the service. My father was half Portuguese. He was a dark skinned man with very black curly hair. My mother was a full blooded Choctaw Indian. When I was discharged from the Army I went right down to St Marks, Fla. and shipped as Cook in the U.S.S Geo. McCollum. She ran between Tortugas, Key West, and New Orleans. I was on her four months. I left her at Key West and shipped

---

[9] This person's name has various spellings throughout the documents. Whether this is from errant memories of the deponent or the examiner's poor spelling is unknown.

on a Rig and went to Liverpool and returned immediately to New York and Key West. I stopped at Key West about four months and then went to Manatee Co. That was down about Pine Level. I went there in 1868 and staid (sic) there until 1870. I worked for H.H. DeCoster until 1869 and then worked for a man named Platt. (Wm Platt) He is dead now. I left there in 1872 and came to this county and have been living right around in The Ten Thousand Islands Islands ever since July 1872. When I left the Army I got a Discharge paper. I lost that aboard the steamer Geo. McCullum. I learned to write since I came to this part of the country. I did not write my name when I went in the Army. I did not sign the pay (rolls), they signed for me and I touched the (pen). I made a claim for pension. I never made a claim for a bounty. I never received any bounty. I do not know a Notary Public named S. Ma____. I never (executed) a claim for bounty before such a man.

My first application for a pension was made a number of years ago. The papers were made out by James Dean. Andrew Anderson is a Schooner Capt hauling wood out of the rivers (?) here. I have known Anderson ever since 1873. He has always known me as Richard Hamilton. I told him my Army name. This was when he identified me, that is all he knows. My last claim for a pension was one year ago. That was written by Judge Phipps. I do not know his initials. I never seen him before the time

I made my claim. Somebody told me about him, and I went to him and asked him if he was Judge Phipps and he said yes. All he knows about my name is what I told him at that time. I know so many Johnsons. I do not know Johnson by the name F.W. Johnson. I know Geo. G. Brooks. Personally, I have known him about a year. He never knew me from ___ _____ until last year sir. There is one man in Key West named John Fletcher who knows me by both names. He did not know me in the Army. There is no person on earth who knows me by both names. I could not give you any name of any person who knew me as Stephen Barrett. I knew a man named Thompson, he was 1st Duty Sgt. of Co. B 99th Regt. The Sgt. Major was Charles Carrol. I am sure I have got my Regt. correct. I can swear positively that I am the identical man who enlisted in Co.G. 99th Regt. U.S. Colored Troops and who served as a soldier under the name.

      Stephen Barrett. "(List of comrades read to witness)"

Q. If any of the names are familiar to you and would know you as Stephen and Richard Hamilton, please... Designate them by names.

_____ that is our Col. He knew me as Barrett, he didn't know me by Hamilton. He was the leading officer of the field. I knew a Sgt. Rudolph. He knew me quite well. He was almost always in some other occupation around with the officers, he did not stay in Camp much. I do not remember P__ J. Smalley, or Lt Small, but the name is somewhat familiar. I remember Hutchinson, I don't remember whether he was Lieut or not. I remember Robert Liggins, he was my _____. I remember Louis Bennett, he belonged to my company. Allen Norris, now of Pensacola Fla. knows me by both names. We had a man in our Co. by name (Jill) Augustine. Aaron Hill was our 2nd Duty Sgt. He never was our Lieut. I remember Augustus Martin, there was two of them, one was named Francis Martin. Anderson Ross was our 1st Duty Sgt. Nelson Shores was drummer... Reddick Wiggins used to be Corporal and was (reduced) to the ranks at Centerville, Fla.

I am a married man. My wife is named Mary. Her maiden name was Mary Weeks. We were married at Key West, Fla. by Justice of the Peace (Lamer) I do not know what year it was. It has been about (twelve) years. I had been married before. Her name was Elizabeth Moore. She may be living. I do not know. I was never divorced from her. She never was divorced from me that I know of. I suppose she was living when I married Mary. Mary had been married before. His name was Geo. Christian. She left him and then married me. I could not tell you anything about whether they were divorced. He was living when I married her.

I have three children under sixteen years of age. The oldest one, Mary was fourteen the 15th day of this October. She is married to Henry Short. Anne Eliza is next to Mary and she was nine years old the 15th of last August. The youngest is Mary Agnes, will be six years old the 2nd day of next month. They are children by my last wife, Mary Weeks. It does not make any difference to me about being present when the testimony is taken. I have fully understood all your questions. My answers have been correctly recorded. I claim my pension on account of a rupture incurred in the service. That happened at the Natural Bridge fight the fall of 1864. I could not rightly say what month. It happened on our retreat, on a double quick march. I did not go to the Hospital. After the engagement was over I complained of being sick and took some medicine, but the Doctor did not examine me. I never told the doctor that I was ruptured. I shared it to half a dozen of the soldiers. I do not know now who they were. The rupture is on the right side, the lower part of the groin. I do not wear a truss. I have had my foot hurt since the war. I have not had any other hurt. I never got hurt before the war. I can't name anyone who knows that I was ruptured in the service. I have fully understood all your questions. My answers have been correctly recorded. I cannot write my name Stephen Barrett.

                Richard Hamilton,
        Stephen X (his mark) Barrett

(Additional signature. A.N. Win____)

Sworn to and subscribed before me this 18th day of Oct 1902 and I certify that the contents were fully made known to deponent before signing.

                J. A. Davis
                      Special Examiner.

DEPOSITION O
Stephen Barrett alias Richard Hamilton

October 18, 1902 St Joseph's Island, Fla.

CLAIMANT'S STATEMENT

DEPOSITION O

Case of Stephen Barrett. No. 996.404

On the eighteenth day of October 1902 at St Joseph's Island, county of Monroe, State of Florida, before me, J. A. Davis, a special examiner of the Bureau of Pensions, personally appeared Stephen Barrett alias Richard Hamilton, the applicant in the aforesaid pension claim, who says:

Q. If it should become necessary to further examine your claim, by taking testimony of witnesses elsewhere, do you desire to be present in person or be represented by an attorney, or both, at such further examination? If so, you will be notified as to the place and time when it is to be made.

A. I could not be present, it is impossible for me to get there. I do not care to be represented.

Q. Should you change your mind and desire to be present, or be represented by an attorney during any further examination of your case, will you *at once* address a letter to the "Commissioner of Pensions, Washington D.C." giving the name and the number of your claim, informing him that you have so changed your mind, and desire to be notified when your claim is to be further examined?

A. Yes sir.

Q. State the names of the person or persons instrumental in the prosecution of your claim for pension, and their post-office addresses.

A. Mr. Nelson was the first man, then James Dean, Judge Phipps, all of Key West Fla. My Atty in Washington ___ Spalding and Co.

Q. State what contract or contracts you have made with such person or persons for their services in prosecuting your claim for pension, and whether such contract or contracts were written or verbal.

A. I never made any contract with, Nelson, Dean or Phipps.

Q. State the amount of fees paid by you or at your instance, to whom paid, and all the circumstances connected with the transaction.

A. I never made any contracts. I paid Dean Some dollars. I have not paid anyone else.

Q. Please give me the names of all witnesses that you desire examined elsewhere, where their post-office addresses, and also state what you expect to prove by each witness.

A. I would like to have Fletcher's testimony of Key West. I do not know of any besides those I have already mentioned before.

Q. Have you any complaint to make as to the conduct, manner, or fairness of the examination of your claim. If so, please state specifically what it is.

(blank answer)

Do you desire to introduce any more testimony before me?

(blank answer)

Attest

A. _____

        Richard Hamilton
        Stephen Barrett
            by his mark
                Deponent

Sworn to and subscribed before me this 18th day of Oct 1902 and I certify that the contents were fully made known to deponent before signing.

        J. A. Davis
           Special Examiner.

DEPOSITION F
Nathan H. DeCoster

October 22, 1902 Punta Gorda, Fla.

Case of Stephen Barrett, No. 996.404

On this twenty second day of Oct, 1902, at Punta Gorda, county of De Soto State of Florida, before me, J. A. Davis, a special examiner of the Bureau of Pensions, personally appeared Nathan H. DeCoster, who, being by me first duly sworn to answer truly all interrogatories propounded to him during this special examination of aforesaid claim for pension, deposes and says:

I am 66 years of age. A fruit grower by occupation and my post office address is, Harbor View, De Soto Co., Fla.

I do not know now, and I have never known any person by the name of Stephen Barrett.

I know and had in my employ for three or four years, a man named Richard Hamilton, from about 1867 to about 1871. I first employed him at Key West Fla., to come over here and work for us. He was a boy then about eighteen or nineteen years old, I should judge. He was a light complexion, about an Octaroon color, a smart active intelligent boy. He was about 5 ft 10 in tall, rather slim built. (He) hair was straight black hair, a little bit curly, but not kinky at all. I do not seem to remember what if any history he gave me as to where he was from, or what he had been doing. He never claimed to have been a soldier. I had another man, John L____ , who claimed to have been in the Navy. He died last year. Hamilton claimed to have been a slave. He married Hannah Moore, a white woman, while he was with me. I have not seen Richard Hamilton since he left me in 1871, or 1872. There were three or four colored men I employed at the time I employed Richard Hamilton, but they are all dead. I never saw Hamilton's mother. I am confident that Richard Hamilton was not over nineteen years of age when I first employed him. I am equally as confident he was not ruptured when he was employed by me, I am sure I would have known it, he was active, strong and rugged. I am satisfied he never had been a soldier, or he would have mentioned the fact. I have no interest in this claim. I have fully understood all your questions. My answers have been correctly recorded.

    N. H. DeCoster
     Deponent.

Sworn to and subscribed before me this 22nd day of October 1902, and I certify that the contents were fully made known to deponent before signing.

    J. A. Davis
     Special Examiner

DEPOSITION G
A. Judson Edwards

November 12, 1902 Ocala, Fla.

Case of Stephen Barrett, No. 996.404

On this twelfth day of November, 1902, at Ocala, county of Marion State of Florida, before me, JA Davis, a special examiner of the Bureau of Pensions, personally appeared A. Judson Edwards, who, being by me first duly sworn to answer truly all interrogatories propounded to him during this special examination of aforesaid claim for pension, deposes and says:

I was 66 the 28th of this August past. I was born in 1836. I am a farmer and stock raiser. My post office address is Ocala, Fla.

My father was Wm P. Edwards. He resided in this county for many years, he came from Ga. down here in 1850. I never knew a man named Stephen Barrett. We had a boy named Stephen who died and my Uncle E____ Edwards had a slave named Stephen. He ran off but I do not know what became of him. My father owned a slave named Richard Hamilton. He was born in Savannah in July 1848. My brother Wm (now dead) was born the 10th August 1848 and Richard was about three weeks old when my brother William was born. I was twelve years old when Richard was born.

His mother we called Peggy, she died some time ago. His father was a light mulatto and belonged to Mr. Frederick He____ of Effingham Co. Ga. We came to Fla in Dec. 1850, the 16 day of the month. Richard remained with my father until the spring of 1865.

I served in the Confederate Army in the 2nd Fla. Cav, but did not leave the State and I was home frequently during the time and the boy Richard was right there on the farm all the time. I got home the 19th May 1865 and Richard was there for some days after I got there. I know the morning he left I had him to help feed the stock and talked with him and then went into breakfast and Richard went off with a __ knock kneed ___ boy named Abram who belonged to a man named Brooks. The next we heard of Richard he was at Key West.

When we got a letter from him a number of years later he wrote he was married and on one of the Keys. He wrote for money to come back, he said he would like to come back to this county to live. My father received the letter and my father either read it to me, or I read it. I saw the letter because I know he plead pretty hard to get back, I read the letter myself. Later on his wife came on and staid (sic) with Richards mother old Aunt Peggy. I can swear positively that Richard did not serve in the Army prior to 1865. Richard had a half brother named Jim Morrison and he lived and died in this county. He had three half brothers named Anderson and they were little boys ____ of the war. They were several years younger than Richard.

My father owned Hamp Hamilton, Ellick Adams, Preston Hamilton, Jim Morrison and Richard. Preston ran off to Key West sometime before Richard did. The others are all dead. I know that Richard did not live in La or go there in 1862. The only John Edwards was my brother and he was with me in the Confederate service. He went in the Army in 1861 and served until 1865. He never was in La. in his life.

He died six years ago here in this county, at the old Homestead. When Richard left here in 1865 he was stout healthy boy. He did not have any rupture, or other ailments, he was perfectly well. I remember that I had Richard cooking for myself and brother John, some of the time while we were in the Army.

I have fully understood all your questions. My answers have been correctly recorded..

        A. J. Edwards, Deponent.

Sworn to and subscribed before me this 12th day of November 1902, and I certify that the contents were fully made known to deponent before signing.

        J.A. Davis, Special Examiner

DEPOSITION E
Richard Hamilton

November 17, 1902 Key West

Case of Stephen Barrett, No. 996.404

On this seventeenth day of November, 1902, at Key West, county of Monroe State of Florida, before me, J. A. Davis, a special examiner of the Bureau of Pensions, personally appeared Stephen Barrett alias Richard Hamilton, who, being by me first duly sworn to answer truly all interrogatories propounded to him during this special examination of aforesaid claim for pension, deposes and says:

I am the identical person who made a statement before you last month, at St (Josephs) Island, relating to my claim for a pension.

Q. You swore that you were a soldier in Co. G 99th Regt. U.S.C. Troops enlisted the last of 1862, or first of 1863, is that correct?

A. That is right, that is correct.

Q. You stated that you were a son of Wm Edwards and that you went with a half brother, John Edwards, to New Orleans, La. during the war, is that correct?

A. Yes sir, I did that.

Q. Was John a son of Wm Edwards?

A. Yes sir, he is dead and gone now and there is no one to say whether it is so, or not.

Q. Did you have any other half brothers?

A. Yes sir, Joseph and Judson Edwards. Joseph was living the last time I heard anything and Judson went crazy.

Q. Did you ever go back to Mr. Edwards after you left in 1862?

A. I never went back there after I left them in 1862 or 1863.

Q. You were never there after the war?

A. No sir, I never appeared to none of them.

Q. Do you know whether any of your half brothers were in the Confederate Army?

A. Yes sir, two of them, John and Judson.

Q. Is this the same John who went with you to New Orleans?

A. Yes sir.

Q. He did not enlist in the Union Army?

A. No sir.

Q. Were you ever in the Confederate Army?

A. No sir.

Q. Did you ever go with John or Judson as cook?

A. No sir.

Q. Is your mother's name Peggy Anderson?

A. She goes by the name Anderson now, but I don't know her husband.

Q. Did you ever know (Abram) Brooks?

A. No sir. I knew a man here named (Irving) Brooks. I do not know where he came from.

Q. Did you ever know Preston Hamilton?

A. No sir.

Q. Did you ever know Ellick Adams, or Jim Morrison?

A. No sir, I don't know them.

Q. Didn't they used to belong to Wm Edwards?

A. I don't know — you got me kind of bothered.

Q. Have you got a sister living?

A. Never that I knew of.

Q. Did you ever have any sisters?

A. Never that I knew of.

Q. Did you ever know C.C. Rawls?

A. No sir. I beg your pardon I knew a Wm Rawls after I went to Manatee Co, but I knew them after I went there in 1868, or 1869.

Q. Who made out your application for a pension?

A. The last one was made out by Mr. Phipps.

Q. You (was) sworn to it before Mr. Phipps?

A. Yes sir, I testified before him that I belonged to the 99th Regt. I told him that I could prove I was in the 99th Regt.

Q. You signed that application Stephen Barrett, by mark?

A. Yes sir.

Q. Who mailed the paper to Washington?

A. I left it with Judge Phipps to mail.

Q. What were the names of your half sisters?

A. Eliza, Ann, Henrietta and (Francis).

Q. Did you have a sister named Matilda?

A. I don't know any such person.

I have fully understood your questions. My answers have been correctly recorded.

Geo. G. Brooks of Key West Fla., hereby certify that the written deposition was read to deponent, that he signed the same by mark, was sworn to in my ----

    Geo. G. Brooks

    Stephen X (his mark) Barrett
alias Richard Hamilton.
        Deponent.

Sworn to and subscribed before me this 17th day of November 1902, and I certify that the contents were fully made known to deponent before signing.

    J.A. Davis

    Special Examiner

DEPOSITION L
J. M. Phipps

November 17, 1902 Key West

Case of Stephen Barrett, No. 996.404

On this seventeenth day of November, 1902, at Key West, county of Monroe State of Florida, before me, J. A, Davis, a special examiner of the Bureau of Pensions, personally appeared J. M. Phipps, who, being by me first duly sworn to answer truly all interrogatories propounded to him during the special examination of aforesaid claim for a pension, deposes and says:

I am 69 years of age.. An Atty at Law and also a Notary Public. My post office address is, Key West, Fla.

I do not know Stephen Barrett personally. I ___ such a man came before me once to execute a claim for a pension. I had never seen him before, that I remember. I do not know anybody by the name of Richard Hamilton, I have understood that the man Stephen Barrett went by that name, but I do not know it. I think I might recognize the man if I should see him.

Q. Signature J. M. Phipps, Notary Public to affidavit signed, Stephen Barrett by mark, dated Oct 9th, 1901, witnessed by F. W. Johnson and Geo G. Brooks and filed in the Pension Office Oct 14, 1901, shown to witness. Is the signature shown to you in your handwriting?

A. Yes that is my handwriting. The writing in the body of that Declaration for Invalid Pension is mine, I filled it up according to his statement made to me at the time. He signed that paper by mark. The declaration was read to him and he was made familiar with the contents. He was sworn to the contents thereof. I think I mailed the paper for him. It was sent to Harry (Harvey?) Spalding and Sons of Washington D.C. I have no further knowledge relating to this claim and I do not know anything about it except as stated to me by the man who represented himself as Stephen Barrett.

My answers have been correctly recorded.

J. M. Phipps

Sworn to and subscribed before me this 17th day of November 1902 and I certify that the contents were fully made known to deponent before signing.

J.A. Davis
Special Examiner

DEPOSITION M
George G. Brooks

November 17, 1902 Key West

DEPOSITION M

Case of Stephen Barrett, No. 996.404

On this seventeenth day of November, 1902, at Key West, county Of Monroe, State of Florida, Before me, J. A. Davis, a special examiner of the Bureau of Pensions, personally appeared Geo. G. Brooks, who, being by me first duly sworn to answer truly all interrogatories propounded to him during this special examination of aforesaid claim for pension, deposes and says:

I am 26 years of age. An Atty at law and post office address is, Key West, Fla. I do not know Stephen Barrett personally, but the name sounds familiar. I know a man named Richard Hamilton who lives up on one of the Keys. I cannot remember whether I have ever witnessed any papers for Stephen Barrett. I would know my signature if I should see it. (Signature, Geo. G. Brooks as attesting witness to Deposition for Invalid Pension, dated Oct 9, 1901, signed Stephen Barrett by mark executed before J.W. Phipps, Notary Public and filed in the Pension Office Oct 14, 1901, shown to witness)

Q. Is the signature shown to you in your handwriting?

A. That is my signature. I signed it as attesting witnesses to his mark.

Q. *Signature as identifying witness to _____ declaration shown to witness.* Is that signature Geo G. Brooks in your handwriting?

A. Yes sir that is in my handwriting. I know the man's face, but do not ____ with regard to his name as he claimed that to be his name.

Q. Do you remember whether the man you know as Richard Hamilton is the man who signed that declaration, Stephen Barrett, by mark?

A. I do not remember that, if I could see the man I would remember.

Q. Have you fully understood all my questions?

A. Yes

Q. Have I set down your answers correctly?

A. Yes sir. The man I testified I had known for two years, I did not know his name, but remembered his face and he told me Stephen Barrett was his name.

Geo. G. Brooks

Sworn to and subscribed before me this 17th day of Nov. 1902, Andy I certify that the contents were fully made known to deponent before signing.

   J. A. Davis
     Special Examiner.

DEPOSITION N
F. W. Johnson

November 18, 1902 Key West

Case of Steven Barrett alias Richard Hamilton, No. 996,404

On this 18th day of November 1902, at Key West, County of Monroe, State of Fla, before me, J. A. Davis, a special examiner of the Bureau of Pensions, personally appeared F. W. Johnson, who, being by me first duly sworn to answer truly all interrogatories propounded to him during the special examination of aforesaid claim for pension, deposes and says:

I am 60 years of age. I am Officer Dep U.S. Marshall. My post office address is Key West Florida.

I know a man named Richard Hamilton who also claims that his name is Stephen Barrett. The first I ever knew that he claimed to be Stephen Barrett was when he made a claim for a pension, before Judge J.M. Phipps. I think it was last year sometime. I had known him as Richard Hamilton a good many years. I remember being called in as a witness to attest his mark when he made his application. I identified him as Stephen Barrett, on his say so. I knew him as Hamilton

Q. *Signature F.W. Johnson as attesting witness and signature F.W. Johnson as identifying witness to "Declaration for Invalid Pension" signed Stephen Barrett, by mark, executed before J.M. Phipps, Notary Public and filed in the Pension Office Oct 14, 1901, shown to witness.* Are the signatures shown to you in your handwriting?

A. Yes, both signatures shown to me are in my handwriting. I saw Hamilton make his mark as Stephen Barrett. I do not know whether he was sworn, and I do not know what was done with the paper after it was completed, I was called in from my office simply as attesting witness and to identify Hamilton who said his name was Stephen Barrett. I have no interest whatsoever in this claim. I have fully understood all your questions. My answers have been correctly recorded.

   F. W. Johnson

Sworn to and subscribed before me this 18th day of November 1902 and I certify that the contents were fully made known to deponent before signing.

   J. A. Davis Special Examiner

DEPOSITION H
Ellick Anderson

November 21, 1902 Elmwood, Fla.

Case of Stephen Barrett, No. 996.404

On this 21st day of November, 1902, at Elmwood, County of Marion State of Florida, before me, J. A. Davis, a special examiner of the Bureau of Pensions, personally appeared Ellick Anderson, who, being by me first duly sworn to answer truly all interrogatories propounded to him during this special examination of aforesaid claim for pension, he deposes and says:

I was born Dec 5, 1852. A farmer by occupation. My post office address is Elmwood, Marion Co, Fla. I was born and raised right here and have always lived here. I knew Wm Edwards and all his people. We did not live no more than a mile and a half apart. I know Richard Hamilton, he belonged to Wm Edwards. I was Richard Hamilton's uncle. Richard is some older than I am, I do not know how much. I was here all during the war. I know that Richard Hamilton was here all during the war, only when he was cooking in the Confederate Army for John and A. J. Edwards. I know that Richard did not go away from here until after the war. After Richard left here he never is been back here. His mother's name was Peggy Anderson. Richard was a slave. He was not married when he was here, he was quite a young lad of a boy. Richard could not have been a soldier in the Union Army, he was not away from here to be a soldier. I never knew a man named Stephen Barrett. After Richard left here, when us heard of him, he was in Key West. I have no interest in this claim. I have fully understood all your questions. My answers have been correctly recorded.

    El Anderson (signature)
    U S Flowers

Sworn to and subscribed before me this 21st day of November 1902 and I certify that the contents were fully made known to deponent before signing.

    J. A. Davis
      Special Examiner

DEPOSITION I
Joseph Edwards

November 21, 1902 Elmwood, Fla.

Case of Stephen Barrett, No. 996. 404

On this twenty first day of November, 1902, at Elmwood, county of Marion State of Florida, before me, J. A .Davis, a special examiner of the Bureau of Pensions, personally appeared Joseph Edwards, who, being by me first duly sworn to answer truly all interrogatories propounded to him during this special examination of aforesaid claim for pension, deposes and says:

I was born Oct 1851. By occupation a farmer. My post office address is Williston, Levy Co. Fla.

I am a son of Wm Edwards. I had brothers, John S. Edwards and A. Judson Edwards and William Edwards. I had sisters, Henrietta, Eliza B. and Elvira. My father owned, Hamp, Preston, James, Ellick, De_____ , Jerry and Richard. Jerry is living, but he was a small boy at the time of the war. I do not know Richards exact age, but he was about three years older than I. He was born a short time before my brother William , who died quite young. I was at home all during the war. I know my brothers John and A.J. Edwards were in the confederate service. I know that

Richard was right here on this place most of the time during the war, except when he was cooking for my brothers. I saw him in camp with them, he and I went there together once and I left him there with them. His mother's name was Peggy. She died not long ago. I know positively that Richard did not go away from here until after the war, I do not know just the month, but it was in 1865. He never has been back here since, at least I have never seen him. His mother has lived about here and I understand has heard from him. I heard that Richard was in Key West, after he left here. I never knew him by any name but Richard Hamilton. I never knew a man named Stephen Barrett.

I have no interest in this claim. I have fully understood all your questions. My answers have been correctly recorded.[10]

Joseph N. Edwards

---

[10] (marked "over" but the next page 24 is missing)

DEPOSITION K
Henrietta E. Jones

November 21, 1902 Elmwood, Fla.

Case of Stephen Barrett, No. 996.404

On this twenty first day of November, 1902, at Elmwood, county of Marion State of Florida, before me, J. A. Davis, a special examiner of the Bureau of Pensions, personally appeared Henrietta E. Jones, who, being by me first duly sworn to answer truly all interrogatories propounded to her during this special examination of aforesaid claim for pension, deposes and says:

I am 57 years of age. I am the widow of D____ Jones. My post office address is Williston, Levy Co. Fla. I never knew any person named Stephen Barrett. I am a daughter of the late Wm Edwards and I was born in Effingham Co, Ga. My father moved to Savannah, Ga. when I was a baby. My father was a slave owner and amongst the number he owned one named Richard Hamilton. Richard was born at Savannah, Ga. He was born the 26th day of July 1848. We had a record of births, but it was burned some years ago. I remember seeing Richard's father very well. He was a very bright mulatto and his hair was almost straight and was said to have Indian blood in his veins. I think his father was named

Richard and that he belonged to Mr. Neece. Richards mother was named Peggy Hamilton and after we came to Florida she married Lou Anderson. We moved to Florida in Dec 1850 and have lived right on this place until 1871. I was at home all during the war. I remember that Richard was here only when he was with my brothers John and A. J. Edwards. They were both in the Confederate service in the 2nd Cav. I know that my brother John never went to New Orleans. My brother John joined the Army in Sept 1861 and before that he was here. After he joined the Army he never left the State. I remember well that Richard was here at the close of the war and that he did not leave here until after my brothers came out of the Army. They came home in May and Richard did not leave before June, or July I know. Richard never came back here, but I read one, or two letters that he wrote back to his mother. I have a sister, Elvira L____ living near G_____, Effingham Co. Ga. She is older than I and she will know about Richards birth and who his father was. I have another sister named Eliza Gra_____ living at Dewey, Duval Co. Fla. who is older than I. She was home some during the war, her husband was in the same Regt and Co. with my brothers. His name is Henry (Graddock).

I have no interest in this claim. I have fully understood all your questions. My answers have been correctly recorded. I

_____ that my father lived on this place after he came from Ga. in (1851), until 1871 and I have lived here on the same place ever since.

    Henrietta E. Jones

Sworn to and subscribed before me this 21st day of November 1902, and I certify that the contents were fully made known to deponent before signing.

    J. A. Davis
      Special Examiner.

Exhibit S, Letter to E. R. Pasley

November 21, 1902 Jacksonville, Fla.

SPECIAL EXAMINATION DIVISION.
Department of the Interior,
Bureau of Pensions, Exhibit S
Jacksonville, Fla,
Nov. 21st, 1902

Dr. E. R. Pasley
Williston, Florida

Dear Sir:

I am informed that you were the family physician for the late Wm P. Edwards, since prior to the civil war (1861-5) and that you also had some service in the 2nd Fla. Cav, C.S.A. Please inform me by endorsement on the back of this letter, whether or not, you remember one "Richard Hamilton" formerly a slave belonging to said Edwards. Whether you remember him during the years said war, on the plantation and in the service as cook for John and A. J. Edwards and whether he was at the plantation at and after the close of the war in 1865 and what became of him. I enclose an addressed return envelope which does not require any stamp. Your early reply will be appreciated.

Very respectfully
J. A. Davis, Special Examiner

"foul murder has been done by him"

1902 Everglade, Fla.

G. H. WATSON

G. W. STORTER

G. H. WATSON & CO.,

DEALERS IN

DRY GOODS AND GROCERIES

Everglade, Fla. 1902.

___ _____ rumor is _____, foul murder has been done by him and this I say without _____ my past and had this man ever done and served for the country as a Soldier he would have one redeeming feature in ____ _____ to have commanded my sympathy. Report says Steven Barrett, Half blood Indian was a soldier in the USC and died. After which the man Hamilton assumed Barretts name. His history can be traced back to when he was a Slave. His father being his owner, whose name was Edwards. When this man Hamilton ____ his first wife was Robt Hamilton some 39 or 40 years past. When he married wife ___ Richard Hamilton.

And one of his families lives here and the other in Tampa.

I will respectfully state that I am a Union Soldier and Pensioner. My Son Bortr___ Watson runs as Postal Clerk from Jacksonville. And while I am not any relative of the man who chopped the cherry tree. Yet this is what I understand to be fact.

      Respt Yours,
        G. H. Watson

Letter to Thomasville, GA Postmaster Regarding Robert Leggins and Louis Bennet (colored)

October 30, 1902 Jacksonville, Fla.

Department of the Interior,
Bureau of Pensions,

SIR:

Please state, on the back of this letter, whether Robert Leggins and Louis Bennet. (colored) resides within your mail delivery, and if so, at what distance from the post-office, and in what direction. If they do not receive mail at your office, any assistance you may be able to give me in locating them, will be appreciated.

This information is desired for use in a claim for pension, No. 996,404, and it is requested that your reply, in the envelope herewith, be forwarded as soon as possible.

Very respectfully,
J. A. Davis, Special Examiner

THE POSTMASTER,
Thomasville, Ga.

Thomas Hamilton

October 30, 1902 Jacksonville, Fla.

Department of the Interior,
Bureau of Pensions,

Mr. Thomas Hamilton[11]
Sarasota, Fla.

Sir:

Please endorse on the back of this letter the present address of your mother, Elizabeth Moore Hamilton and now as I have been informed McCloud. I desire to see her relating to a pension matter. I enclose an addressed return official envelope which does not require any stamp. Your early reply will be appreciated.[12]

Very respectfully
J. A. Davis
Special Examiner

---

[11] Thomas Hamilton is the son of Richard Hamilton and his first wife, Hannah Moore.

[12] As of Jan 6 1903, this letter was returned marked "unclaimed."

Recommend criminal proceedings

February 2, 1903 Jacksonville, Fla.

DEPARTMENT OF JUSTICE,
WASHINGTON, D. C.

Joseph N. Stripling, Esq.,
U. S. Attorney,

Sir:

I send you the papers in the original claims for pension, #996.404, of Stephen Barrett, and #531.374, of Sarah Barrett, together with a copy of a letter from the Commissioner or Pensions dated the 24th ultimo, Setting forth the evidence of violation of section 5438 revised statutes U. S., on the part of the alleged Steven Barrett, whose name is Richard Hamilton, post office address Key West, Florida, care of John A. Pitcher, but who resides north of Key West upon one of the Island Keys, known as the Ten Thousand Isles, and recommending the institution of criminal proceedings against him therefor.

You are directed to proceed as indicated, unless your examination of the matter shall show good and sufficient reason for not doing so. The papers sent to you are to be returned to this department when they have served their purpose, together with your report of the action taken in the case.

Respectfully, ____ Attorney General

Summary of Depositions

January 24, 1903 Washington, D. C.

3-1868

LAW DIVISION

Department of the Interior,

Summary of Cases Bureau of Pensions,

Washington, D. C. January 24, 1903.

The Honorable,

The Secretary of the Interior.

Sir:

I herewith have the honor to forward the original papers in the claims of Stephen Barrett, alleged late private, Cos. C and G, 99th U. S. C. V. I., Orig. No. 996,404, and of Sarah Barrett, alleging that her deceased husband is the identical person who rendered said service, Orig. No. 531,374, together with reports of Special Examiners Davis, Wiggenhorn, Montgomery and Gilpin relative thereto, for your consideration and reference to the Department of Justice, for transmission to the United States Attorney for the Southern

District of Florida, with a view to the criminal prosecution of the invalid claimant, Stephen Barrett, whose genuine name is Richard Hamilton, and whose post office address is Key West, Monroe County, Florida, % John A. Pitcher, but who actually resides, however some forty miles South (sic) of Key West upon one of the Island Keys, known as the Ten Thousand Isles, for violation of the provisions of section 5438, Revised Statutes of the United States.

HISTORY.

The invalid claimant, Richard Hamilton, alias Stephen Barrett, first filed a declaration January 27, 1891. This claim was rejected November 26, 1899, on the ground that he failed to prove that he was identical with the soldier who rendered the service. The widow claimant filed her claim November 6, 1891, and a second declaration December 3, 1896. Her claim was rejected August 12, 1899, upon the ground that she was not the legal widow of the deceased soldier, having a living husband from whom she was not divorced at the time of the soldier's death.

The widow claimant, **Sarah Barrett, whose real name is Sarah Miller**, did live for many years with the soldier as his wife, though she, as herinbefore stated, had a living husband from whom she was not divorced throughout the entire period of her association with the soldier. Among other papers filed by her is the original discharge certificate granted to the soldier of this service, and which was in the possession of the said Stephen Barrett, with whom she lived as his wife at the time of his death, which had been in his possession constantly after his discharge from the service. The genuine soldier according to this discharge certificate and according to the records of the War Department was 25 years of age at the time he enlisted, August 20, 1863; was five feet, six inches high and was black--in every respect an African. The contesting invalid claimant, Richard Hamilton, alias Stephen Barrett, of Key West, Florida, is light in color, an octoroon, over six feet tall as shown by the evidence herewith set forth was about 19 years of age in 1868 or 1869--four years after the close of the civil war.

The evidence upon which this recommendation is based is briefly set forth as follows:

Isom Anthony, of Killons, Saint Charles Parish, Louisiana, in a deposition before Special Examiner J. W. Montgomery, states that he served in Cos. H and C, 99th U. S. C. V. I.; that he was acquainted with one Stephen Barrett, who served in Cos. G and C of the same regiment; that deponent met him in said service; that the said Barrett was about five feet, six inches tall, was black in color, with black hair and eyes and weighed about one hundred and fifty pounds; was fully grown; that deponent and the said Stephen Barrett settled in Saint Charles Parish after service and deponent knew him well from that time until the time of his death; that at the time of his death he was living with a woman by the name of Sarah as his wife.

Exhibit 3, page 23 of the report of **Special Examiner A. C. Wiggenhorn,** is the original discharge certificate granted by Captain Frank D. Harding to Stephen Barrett as a member of Co. C, setting forth the fact that he was duly enlisted in said company of the 99th U. S. C. V. I., on the 20th day of August, 1863, and honorably discharged therefrom on April 23, 1866, at Tallahassee, Florida--services being no longer required; that he was born in Virginia, was 25 years of age at the time of enlistment; five feet, six inches high, with black complexion, black eyes, and black hair.

The **records of the War Department** show that there was but one soldier by the name Stephen Barrett who rendered service in Companies C and G, 99th U. S. C. V. I.; that he was mustered into Co, G, 99th U. S. C. V. I., August 20, 1863, and mustered out April 23, 1866, as of Co. C, said Reg., to which he was transferred December 8, 1865.

Special Examiner J. A. Davis, who may be addressed Commissioner of Pensions, Washington, D. C., is competent to testify that on the 18th day of October, 1902, Richard Hamilton, alias Stephen Barrett, the original invalid claimant for pension as member of Cos. C and G, 99th U. S. C. V. I., stated to him that the claimant was a slave; that he was born in Savannah, Georgia; that his mother was named Peggy Hamilton, owned by one William Edwards who was claimant's father; that the said William Edwards moved from Savannah, Georgia, to Marion County, Florida, together with his family and his slaves, including the claimant, Richard Hamilton, alias Stephen Barrett; that the said William Edwards had several children, John, Joseph and Judson; that John is dead; Judson is crazy and Joseph is living somewhere in Florida; that claimant, Richard Hamilton, alias Stephen Barrett, in 1863, left the home of William Edwards, in Marion County, Florida, together with his half-brother, John Edwards and proceeded to Louisiana where the claimant enlisted in Co. G, 99th U. S. C. V. I., and served in the same until he was transferred to Co. C, and discharged therefrom.

Judson Edwards, of Ocala, Marion County, Florida, before Special Examiner Davis states that he is the son of William Edwards, who resided in Marion County, Florida for many years before his death; that deponent's father prior to 1850, when he came to Marion County, Florida, lived in Savannah, Georgia; that among other slaves owned by him was one Richard Hamilton, who was born in Savannah in July, 1848; that Richard Hamilton's mother was named Peggy and she was also owned by deponent's father; that Richard Hamilton remained with deponent's father until the spring of 1865; that deponent served in the Confederate army, in the 2d Florida Calvary, but did not leave the State of Florida and was at home frequently during his service in said organization and that the boy, Richard Hamilton, was throughout the entire period upon deponent's father's place in Marion County, Florida, with the exception of a short while when he cooked for deponent and his brother John, who was also a member of the 2d Florida Cavalry, Confederate States Army; that he did not leave the farm of deponent's father until sometime in May, 1865--deponent thinks the 19th day of that month; that deponent remembers distinctly incidents connected with the morning that the said Richard Hamilton left his father's home; that the said Richard Hamilton went to Key West, Florida, where he has continued to reside ever since; that some years after he left deponent's father, he received a letter from Richard Hamilton, begging that money be sent him to come back to Marion County, Florida, stating that he desired to come there and live; that Richard Hamilton's mother, Peggy Hamilton, lived upon the place of deponent' father until the day of her death and was buried by deponent's family; that deponent's brother John was never in the State of Louisiana in his life, nor was

Richard Hamilton ever in said State until after May, 1865, and not then to the knowledge of deponent; that said Richard Hamilton was never known as Stephen Barrett to deponent's knowledge and was never a member of the Federal army or navy; that he was never old enough to have been a member of either during the war.

Ellick Anderson, of Elmwood, Marion County, Florida, in a deposition before Special Examiner Davis, states that he is well acquainted with Richard Hamilton, who belonged as a slave to one William Edwards, who lived in Savannah, Georgia, until 1850, when he moved to Marion County, Florida and lived until the day of his death; that deponent is an uncle of the said Richard Hamilton; that the said Richard Hamilton is a son of Peggy Hamilton, who was also a slave of Mr. William Edwards; that Richard Hamilton, at the time of the Civil War was nothing but a boy; that he was not absent from William Edwards' place in Marion County, Florida, for any period whatsoever, other than a short time that he was cooking for William Edwards' two sons, John and A. J. Edwards, who were Confederate soldiers in a Florida organization, which did not leave the State; that Richard Hamilton did not leave Marion County, Florida, other than to cook for the aforesaid John and A. J. Edwards, until after May 1865.

Joseph Edwards of Elmwood, Marion County, Florida, in a deposition before

Special Examiner Davis, states that he is a son of William Edwards; that he had brothers by the name of John and Judson Edwards and a sister by the name of Henrietta; that deponent's father, prior to 1850, lived in Savannah, Georgia, and owned slaves, among whom were Peggy Hamilton and a son of hers, Richard by name; that Richard and Peggy Hamilton were brought by members of the family to Marion County, Florida, and Peggy lived with the family until the day of her death, several years ago; that Richard Hamilton was nothing more than a boy during the Civil War and was not absent from deponent' father's place, in Marion County, Florida, during the Civil War or any time whatsoever other than a short period, when he was cooking for deponent's brothers, John and Judson, who were members of the Confederate Cavalry organization, known as the 2d Florida, which did not go outside of the confines of the State of Florida.; Deponent saw Richard Hamilton cooking for his brothers in said camp; that the said Richard Hamilton did not leave Marion County permanently until after the close of the Civil War, when he settled in Key West, Florida, and has continued to reside there since.

Henrietta E. Jones, of Elmwood, Marion County, Florida, in a deposition before Special Examiner Davis, states that she is a daughter of William Edwards, who, until 1850, resided in Savannah, Georgia, when he moved to Marion County, Florida, where he lived until the day of his death, some years ago; that the said William Edwards was possessed of several slaves-- among them Peggy Hamilton, a son of hers, Richard Hamilton, born July, 1848. These two, Peggy and Richard Hamilton, were brought to Marion County, Florida, with the family, in 1850, and Peggy remained with them until the day of her death, several years ago. Richard remained with the family until he went to Key West, Florida, to live, in 1865, after the Civil War; was on the place in Marion County, Florida, throughout the entire period of the Civil War, except for a short time when he was cooking for two of deponent's brothers, John and A. Judson Edwards, who were members of the 2d Florida Cavalry, Confederate Army; that the said Richard Hamilton was thus cooking for John and Judson Edwards but a very short time, however; that he was not a member of any Federal military organization, because he was not long enough absent from deponent's home to have been a member of any military establishment and within the short time he was absent from said home his absence was fully accounted for and his habits known by reason of the fact that he was cooking for the aforesaid John and Judson Edwards.

J. M. Phipps, of Key West, Monroe county, Florida, in a deposition before the Special Examiner Davis, states that he is an attorney-at-law and a notary public; that he is not acquainted personally with one Stephen Barrett, but that he does know by sight, a Negro man, who executed a claim for pension before deponent under the name of Stephen Barrett; that what purports to be deponent's signature to the jurat of a declaration purporting to have been executed by Stephen Barrett, October 9, 1901, in the presence of F. W. Johnson, and George G. Brooks as attesting and identifying witnesses, and filed in the Bureau of Pensions October 14, 1901, is in fact deponent's genuine signature and the paper was executed as it purports; that said paper was prepared by deponent at the dictation of the said Stephen Barrett, after which Stephen Barrett signed the same by mark and subscribed to the oath administered to him by deponent in the presence of attesting and identifying witnesses.

George G. Brooks, of Key West, Florida, in his deposition before Special Examiner Davis, states that he is an attorney-at-law; that he has no personal acquaintance with one Stephen Barrett, but that he is well acquainted with one Richard Hamilton, a Negro who lives some miles South of Key West, on one of the Florida Island Keys; that what purports to be deponent's signature as an attesting and identifying witness to a declaration executed by Stephen Barrett, October 9, 1901, in the presence of George G. Brooks and F. W.

Johnson, before J. M. Phipps, a notary public, and filed in the Bureau of Pensions, October 14, 1901, is in fact deponent's genuine signature; said paper was executed by the person deponent knows as Richard Hamilton, who alleged that his army name was Stephen Barrett.

F. W. Johnson, of Key West, Florida, in a deposition before Special Examiner Davis, states that he is Deputy United States Marshal, located in Key West; that his signature as an attesting and identifying witness to a declaration purporting execution by Stephen Barrett, before J. M. Phipps in the presence of deponent and George G. Brooks, is in fact deponent's genuine signature; that deponent does not know the claimant as Stephen Barrett at all, but does know him as Richard Hamilton; that he stated that he sought pension under the name of Stephen Barrett, because he rendered service under that name, at the time of the execution of his declaration.

Inasmuch as the Statute of Limitations prevent criminal proceedings in connection with the first declaration filed by Richard Hamilton, alias Stephen Barrett, the proceedings herein recommended, if instituted, must be based upon the declaration executed October 9, 1901, and filed October 14, 1901. The records of this Bureau do not show the filing of any but the first declaration and there are no certified copies of record by which the actual filing of this declaration can be shown, as provided for in section 882, Revised Statutes of the United States.

In event criminal proceedings are instituted, as hereinbefore recommended, the foregoing witnesses, whose addresses have been given, or such of them as may be deemed expedient by the United States Attorney, should appear in behalf of the Government, and a subpoena duces tecum should issue addressed to the Secretary of War, directing him or some employs of that Department designated by him in his stead to produce the original roll of Companies C and G, 99th U. S. C. V. I., to show that there was but one soldier who rendered service in either of said organizations under the name Stephen Barrett and he was transferred from one organization to the other, and his personal description.

Very respectfully,

J. L. _____

Acting Commissioner.

Form No. 15.

PRECIPE FOR SUBPOENA IN A CASE

In the District Court, United States, La District of Fla

THE UNITED STATES
vs
Lepton Barnett

The Clerk of said Court will issue Subpoena for the following-named persons to appear before said Court, at the United States Court Rooms, in Key West, at 9 o'clock, A. M., on the _____ day of May, 190_, then and there to testify in behalf of the United States.

NAMES	RESIDENCE
Frank Miller (church Smith)	Killarn, St Charles Parish, La
Sam Anthony	Killarn, St Jefferson Ann Du Dries, La
Andrew Edwards	Pecan, Fla
John Phipps	Key West
Geo. E. Porter	Key West
Elliott Anderson	Elwood, Marion Co., Fla
La_ward	

This _____ day of _____, 1910.

Geo. B. Pasley Jr. Williston, Fla.

_____ U. S. Attorney.

Accused is indicted

June 23rd, 1904 Washington DC

Department of the Interior Bureau of Pensions

Auditor for War Department,
US Treasury,

Sir:

In response to your letter of the ninth ___, enclosed herewith, requesting information with reference to the claim of Stephen Barrett, late of C 99 U.S.C.I, I have to state that Sarah Barrett was an applicant for pension as the Widow of Stephen Barrett late of C & G 99th USCI, 0.531, 374, and that one Richard Hamilton of Key West, Florida, filed an application under the allegation that he is the _____ Stephen Barrett who performed said service, No. 996, 404.

These claims were investigated, and it was shown to the satisfaction of this Bureau the genuine Steven Barrett is dead, and that Richard Hamilton did not serve as alleged under the name of Steven Barrett, nor was he otherwise in the military service of the US.

On May 7th, 1903, the accused was indicted and the papers pertaining to both claims are now in the hands of the US District Attorney. He reports that his failure to try the case is chargeable to the fact that the Marshall has not been able to locate and arrest the defendant. If there has been filed in your office a claim of any character by the man who resided at Key West Florida, I would appreciate your courtesy if you would return this letter with a certified copy of all papers on file in the claim, to the end that the case may be transmitted to the US District Attorney for use ____ against the accused.

It is understood that this man resides on a small island, some ____ from Key West, and in a very inaccessible location.

     Very respectfully,

     _____

     Acting Commissioner

Treasury Department,
OFFICE OF THE
AUDITOR FOR THE WAR DEPARTMENT,

June 28, 1904:

Respectfully returned to the
Hon. Commissioner of Pensions.

The records of this office show that in the case of Stephen Barrett, late Pvt., Co. C, 99th U. S. C. Inf., pay from August 20 to December 31, 1863, and $200 bounty, Acts of July 22, 1861, and July 28, 1866, were allowed to the soldier by Treasury Certificate No. 393,305, issued January 29, 1868. The claim was filed December 6, 1866, and claimant's post office address was given as follows: "Algiers, Parish of Orleans, R. B., in the State of Louisiana".

Another claim was filed May 26, 1904, in this office, for arrears of pay and bounty, by Stephen Barrett of Everglade, Fla., as late Pvt., Co. G, 99th U. S. C. I., and said claim is now undergoing examination the claimant was identified in the last above mentioned claim by F. W. Johnson and George G. Brooks, both residing in Key West, Fla., and the application was sworn to before J. M. Phipps, notary Public, Monroe Cunty, Fla

The name of Richard Hamilton does not appear in the evidence on file in either of the claims above mentioned.

If a copy of all the testimony filed in support of each of the claims referred to above is desired, please renew the call. No claim has been filed in the case of Richard Hamilton, as of the aforesaid service.

>   __ Rittencen
>   Auditor.

By Chief, Records Division.

Orig. 531,374
B.I. 265,449:

Fugitive from Justice

October 21, 1921 Washington, D. C.

Exhibit A 2

Law Division
Department of the Interior
Bureau of Pensions
Washington DC

Chief of the special examination division

Sir:

Relative to the case of the United States versus John Leyghton alias Doc Leighton and Cyrus H. Hicks of Jacksonville, Florida, for violation of the provisions of the act of April 18th, 1884, the United States Attorney at Jacksonville, Florida, under date of the 15th instant, states in reply to Bureau letter calling for the status of a case that the same has been nolle prossed, inclosing(sic) with his reply a report dated October 16th, 1908 of Special Examiner J. A. Davis, regarding the case of Thomas McDonald alias Tomlin and several miscellaneous papers, and further stating that these were all the papers in his files.

Under date of November 27th, 1908 Special Examiner J. A. Davis turned over seven reports on the above-cited case to United States Attorney J. H. Cheney, taking his receipt therefor.

The papers and the claim of Sarah Barrett, widow of Stephen Barrett, Company C, 99 United States Colored Infantry, Original No. 531374, and in the contesting claim of Richard Hamilton alias Stephen Barrett, original No. 996404, were in the hands of the United States Attorney for the Southern District of Florida for the purpose of prosecuting Richard Hamilton Alias Steven Barrett who was indicted May 7th, 1903 at Key West for violation of section 5438, R.S.U.S. Hamilton became a fugitive from justice and never was apprehended. In June, 1920, the U.S. Attorney nolle prossed the case. He was requested to return the papers in the above-cited claims and replied that they could not be found.

On December 9th, 1920 you were requested by this division to have a special examiner when next at Key West secure or personally make a thorough search at that place for the missing papers.

Special examiner George M. Beckett reported that on June 3, 1921 he called on the deputy Clerk of the United States court at Key West, Florida, who stated that he had no papers pertaining to this case in his office, that all such papers were forwarded to the head office at Jacksonville, and that on June 13th, 1921 he called on the clerk of the United States district court at Jacksonville to search the files of his office and found four papers, copies of which Mr. Becket furnished and that Exhibit C of said four papers seems to have been the only one among those found that was prepared in the Pension Bureau. The four papers in question were merely a part of the indictment found in this case with an attached copy of the Declaration of Steven Barrett made by the accused Richard Hamilton.

The paper is desired to be returned are those in the pension claims of Sarah Barrett and the imposter Richard Hamilton. The papers in both Bob's mentions cases and the Seven special examiner's reports mentioned ought to be in the files of the district attorney I have not been returned to the sparrow and in all probability are stored away instead attorney's office with old records. A special examiner when next in the vicinity of Jacksonville should call upon the district attorney and Endeavor to have, or if possible to make, a personal search for the missing papers-- no matter where they may be stored in or about the District Attorney's office or in the clerk's office or wherever they may have stored old files going back for some years, as the papers in the Barrett claims may have been stored away since 1903. As the papers and such claims were possibly taken to Key West further search should be continued at that place if they are not found at Jacksonville.

Respectfully,
H.P. Willey
Law Clerk.

APPENDIX

Dupart-Barnett Case, The Times-Picayune. New Orleans, Louisiana. Sun, Mar 11, 1894 · Page 3

PENSION FRAUD CASES.

Another Charge Against Dupart and Barnett.

Proceedings were instituted against Dupart and Barnett for pension fraud before Commissioner Wright yesterday.

The affidavit was made against the two men a few days ago by J. W. Montgomery, Esq., of the pension office, and the charge is that Dupart and Barnett conspired together to defraud the government by collecting pensions under the name of Raymond Dennis, a colored soldier, who is now dead.

Judge Morris Marks appeared for Dupart. When the case was called Barnett asked for a severance in the absence of his attorney, Major Armbruster, but it was disallowed on the protest of the government.

Mr. Montgomery on the witness stand said that he had made a full investigation of the case. Dennis was said to have lived at No. 275 Claiborne street, but the vouchers were returned to No. 175 Claiborne, which is the residence of Dupart, one of the accused in this case. Dupart signed all vouchers. The pension was allowed in December, 1892, while Dennis died in October, 1891. It is alleged a number of the names on the claim for Dennis' pension are forgeries. Dennis actually lived in one of the parishes. The papers were introduced in evidence with the name of Notary Barnett upon them. Mr. Montgomery said that Dupart had received checks while Dennis was in his grave.

At this stage of the proceedings Barnett waived further examination and he was committed to the United States circuit court to await the action of the grand jury, being released from custody, however, on his bond for $1000.

The proceedings were temporarily interrupted by the entrance of the deputy United States marshal, who said Dupart was wanted in the United States circuit court, where his bondsmen desired to surrender him. After Dupart returned, Mary Ann Banks, a sister of Dennis, was put on the stand, and her testimony was somewhat in corroboration of the affidavit.

Dupart will probably be bound over to the United States circuit court. There are already pending several cases in that court against him, the offenses being similar to that upon which he was being tried to-day.

3—295.
(Old No. 1—443.)

INDEX
TO SPECIAL EXAMINER'S REPORT.

Claim of Stephen Barrett   No. 996.404

PAGES	NAMES OF WITNESSES, ETC.	Exhibits.	Depositions.	REPUTATION
1 to	Index			
2	Notice to claimant	A.		
7 to 10	Summary			
11 to 15	Claimant's statement		D.	Bad
16, 17	" "		E.	"
	3 Burnn letter, receipts, forwarding papers	B.		
4-6	Law Div. letter Dec 18/91 with instructions	C.		
18-19	Nathan N. De Coster		F.	Excellent
20-21	A. Judson Edwards		G.	"
	22 Ellick Anderson (colored)		H.	Good
23-24	Joseph Edwards		I.	Excellent
25-26	Henrietta C. Jones		K.	"
	27 J. W. Phipps		L.	Good
28-29	Geo. R. Brooker		M.	"
	30 F. W. Johnson		N.	"
31-32	Claimant's final statement		O.	Bad
	33 Mahinjin Thompson, reply to Ci. letter	P.		
34-35	G. K. Holson letter relating to claimants	Q.		Good
36-37	D & C. Purdy - reply to letter	R.		Excellent

221

(

(Graddock)
  Henry, 191
(Grander), 159
(Legham) (Leggins)
  Robert, 160
(Mordagie)
  Dr. Lisha, 119
(Tolinson)
  A. W., 19
(Valcen Mermion's)
  plantation, *123*

A

Abram
  (slave of a man named
    Brooks), 172
Adams
  Alfred, 128
  Ellick, 173, 176
Alexander
  J. K., 102
Anderson. *See* Peggy
  Hamilton, *See* Peggy
  Hamilton
  Andrew, 4, 13, 61, 65,
    66, 69, 75, 78, 161
  Ellick, 4, 186, 188, 206
  Frank E, 2, 58
  Henry, 142
  Lou, 65, 173, 191
  Ross, 142
Anthony
  Isom, 4, 2, 40, 41, 42, 44,
    45, 47, 50, 52, 87, 103,
    117, 118, 156, 160, 202

Augustin
  Julian, 142
Augustine
  (Jill), 163

B

Ballou
  Henry, 88
Barnett
  William B., 21
Barrett
  Sarah, 3, 2, 3, 13, 21, 22,
    35, 36, 40, 42, 44, 45,
    46, 49, 51, 55, 57, 59,
    61, 64, 66, 76, 79, 82,
    83, 85, 87, 89, 94, 100,
    101, 102, 107, 108,
    110, 112, 117, 120,
    121, 123, 127, 130,
    135, 143, 149, 156,
    201, 213, 218
  Stephen, 49, 57, 64, 66,
    102, 103, 218
Beckett
  George M., 1, 218
Bell
  H. C., 58
Bennett
  Louis, 163, 196
Boggs
  B., 3, 41, 103
Brooks
  Abram, 176
  George G., 4, 19, 137,
    162, 178, 179, 181,
    182, 209, 210, 215
  Irving, 176
Brown

George, 41
Bryant
  P. W., 4, 64
Bundy
  C. S., 2, 9, 11, 38
Bushell
  A. M., 32, 34, 39

C

Canady
  W. P., 2, 4, 31, 32, 68
Carrol
  Charles, 162
Cheney
  J. H., 217
Chokoloskee, *69*
Christian
  George, 163
Clark
  John, 159
Cooper
  Paul, 41, 87
Cox
  Milton S., 3, 84, 101, 108, 112, 116, 117, 118, 121, 124, 133
Crickmore
  H. G., 3, 10
Cuddy
  S. A., 2, 105, 157

D

Darensburg
  Adam, 102
Davis
  Hank, 160
  J. A., 73, 76, 91, 96, 149, 150, 154, 165, 166, 168, 170, 173, 178, 179, 181, 183, 184, 186, 188, 190, 196, 203, 217
de Lamar
  Jose, 14, 23
Dean
  James, 13, 30, 49, 51, 61, 65, 66, 68, 70, 71, 73, 161, 167
  Nelson, 4
DeCoster
  Nathan H., 4, 161, 169
Dominique
  Mary T., 3, 22, 45, 46, 47
Dupart
  J. G., 42, 46
Dupart-Barnett case, *50*, 51, *220*

E

Edwards
  A. Judson, 4, 171, 173, 175, 176, 186, 188, 191, 193, 204, 206, 208
  Ann, 177
  Eliza, 177, 188, 191
  Elvira, 188, 191
  Henrietta, 5, 177, 188
  John, 159, 173, 174, 176, 188, *191*, 193, 204, 205, 206
  Joseph N., 4, 158, 175, 188, 189, 204, 206, 207
  Uncle E____., 171
  William, 171, 174, 188
  William Pitts, 158, 171, 175, 176, 186, 188,

190, 193, 194, 204, 206, 207
Effingham Co. Ga., *172*, *190*
Elmwood, Fla., *158*, *186*, *188*, *190*
Elmwood, Marion County, Florida, *206*, *207*
English
  Nelson, 5, 64, 71, 73, 75, 95
Evans
  Hon. H. Clay, 2, 130, 146
Everglades, *19*, 146, *150*, *153*, *154*, *194*, *215*

F

Farror
  T. (Stobo), 2, 38
Ferguson
  C. L., 3, 10
Ferris
  2nd Lieutenant, 159
  Anderson, 159
Fisher
  H., 101
Fletcher, 35
  John, 162

G

G. H. WATSON & CO., *154*, *194*
Gilpin
  C. M., 2, 4, 62, 66, 68, 70, 200
Griffin
  McKensie, 3, 10

H

Hamilton
  Anne Elizabeth, 164
  Hamp, 173, 188
  John, 90, 150, 154
  Mary Agnes, 164
  Peggy, 65, 158, 172, 189, 191, 204, 205, 206, 207, 208
  Preston, 173
  Preston), 176
  Richard (Robert), 3, **5**, 63, 71, 73, 74, 76, 90, 94, 95, 98, 150, 153, 158, 161, 164, 166, 169, 171, 179, 181, 182, 184, 186, 189, 190, 193, 194, 198, 202, 204, 205, 207, 210, 213, 218, 1
  Thomas, 5, 197
Harding
  Captain Frank D., 203
Hardings
  Captain Frank, 5, 6, 8
HARVEY SPALDING & SONS, *19*, *136*
Hicks
  Cyrus H., 217
Hill
  Aaron, 142, 159, 163
Hutchey
  1st Lieutenant, 159
Hutchinson
  Walter H., 142

I

Ingram

Thomas D., 24

J

James
  (slave of William Pitts Edwards), 188
Jefferson
  Perry, 3, 10
Jerry
  (slave of William Pitts Edwards), 188
Johnson
  F. W., 5, 137, 139, 162, 179, 184, 209, 210, 215
Jones. *See* Henrietta Edwards, *See* Henrietta Edwards
Jupter
  Zeno, 80, 101

K

Kelona, Louisiana, *156*
Key West, *4, 5, 12, 13, 26, 27, 30, 49, 51, 57, 58, 59, 60, 61, 64, 65, 66, 68, 69, 71, 72, 73, 76, 89, 94, 98, 136, 137, 139, 141, 144, 146, 151, 154, 158, 162, 163, 167, 169, 172, 173, 174, 178, 179, 181, 184, 187, 189, 198, 201, 202, 205, 207, 208, 209, 210, 213, 214, 215, 218, 219*
Kurtz
  Ida S., 34, 39

L

Labiche
  S. H., 111
Leggins
  Robert, 196
Leggisso
  Robert, 142
Leighton
  Doc, 217
Lewis
  Charles, 22
Lochren
  (Lockhorn) Hon. William, 2, 62, 67
Lyon
  Simon, 115

M

Maden
  A., 101
Madere
  A., 84, 86
Magner
  S., 3, 11, 38
Marion Co., Fla., *158*
Marion County, Florida, *204, 208*
Marshall
  Mary, 119
Martin
  Augustus alias Ogasse, 142
  Augustus., 163
  Francis, 163
  J. B., 3, 96, 101, 102, 104, 109, 112, 118, 121, 131, 132, 156
  Wiiliam, 108

William, 82, 83, 84, 85,
  101, 108, 109, 113,
  115, 118, 131, 132,
  157, 160
William., 3
McCloud. *See* Hannah
  Elizabeth Moore Hamilton
McDonald
  Thomas, 217
Miller
  John, 3, 119, 127, 128,
    160
  Sam, 3, 40, 103, 104, 113,
    114, 118, 119, 120,
    121, 125, 127, 131,
    132, 143, 157
  Sarah (Barrett), 79, 101,
    121, 132, 160, 201
Montgomery
  J. W., 2, 40, 43, 44, 45, 46,
    48, 50, 52, 57, 59, 64,
    96, 103, 125, 131, 200,
    202
Moore
  Captain John, 159
  Hannah Elizabeth, 5,
    163, 170, 197
Morris
  Lee, 120
Morrison
  Jim, 172, 176
Myers
  Thos. J., 3, 11

N

Natural Bridge, *19*, *27*,
  159, *164*
Neece, *191*

New Orleans, *2*, *3*, *8*, *10*,
  21, *38*, *41*, *42*, *45*, *46*, *49*,
  51, *71*, *72*, *74*, *77*, *130*,
  142, *160*, *174*, *175*, *191*,
  220
Norris
  Allen, 163

O

Ocala, Fla., *171*
Orr
  Louis, 119

P

Pasley (Paisley)
  Dr. E. R., 5, 193
Phipps
  J. M., 5, 18, 138, 139, 144,
    147, 161, 162, 167,
    177, 179, 181, 184,
    185, 208, 210, 215
PHIPPS & BROOKS, *146*
Pine Level, Fla., *161*
Pinkney
  Joseph, 76
Pitcher
  John A., 158, 201
Platt
  William, 161
Pleasant Hill, La., *159*
Preston
  (slave of William Pitts
    Edwards), 188
Punta Gorda, Fla., *169*

R

Rawls

C. C., 176
William, 177
Redmond
William A., 22
Reed
Isham (Isom), 3, 102, 104, 108, 118, 123, 131, 133, 157, 160
Richardson
Orderly Sgt, 159
Robbins
A., 102
Roberts
(Bowie), 112, 113
B., 80
James A., 5, 64
Ross
Anderson, 159, 163
Rudolph
Sgt, 162
Ruffin
Rev., 118
Rev. Louis, 88

S

Saint Charles Parish, Louisiana, *202*
Sarah
(slave of William Pitts Edwards), 158
Savannah, Ga., *158, 190*
Savannah, Georgia, *204, 206, 207*
Shores
Nelson, 163
Short
Henry, 164
Mary Hamilton, 164
Smalley
P__ J., 163
Smith
Spencer, 41
Sophia
(slave of William Pitts Edwards), 158
Spalding and Co., *167*
Spalding and Sons, *180*
St John's Parish, Louisiana, *157*
St Joseph's Island, Fla., *166*
St Josephs Island, Fla., *158*
Stephen
(slave of William Pitts Edwards), 171
Stevens
Nelson, 142
Stripling
Joseph N., 2, 198
Swan
Charles, 142
Charley, 159

T

Ten Thousand Islands, *71, 72, 77*, 90, *95, 161, 201*

U

U.S.S Geo. McCollum, *160*

V

Varice
Puppen, 119

Vaucresson
  Edward, 88

W

W. P. CANADAY & CO., *13*
Waddill
  J. J., 128
Walters Jr (Welters)
  Samuel J., 66, 69
Waterford Plantation, *4, 88, 119*
Watson
  G. H., 5, 195
Weeks
  Mary, 163
Wellters Jr
  Samuel J., 5, 61
Whitehead
  Colonel Peter, 4, 42, 47, 83, 101, 103, 107, 109, 115, 118, 123, 156, 160
  Nelson, 4, 82, 83, 84, 85, 96, 101, 102, 104, 107, 110, 113, 118, 120, 123, 131, 132, 157, 160
  Steven, 124
Wiggenhorn
  E. C., 2, 111, 112, 116, 117, 120, 122, 123, 126, 129, 133, 200, 203
Wigginhorn
  E. C., 107
Wiggins
  Reddick, 142, 163
Willey
  H. P., 219
Willis
  Alfred, 102
Williston, Fla, *193*
Williston, Levy Co. Fla., *188, 190*
Wilson
  James, 118

Want to read more about Richard Hamilton?

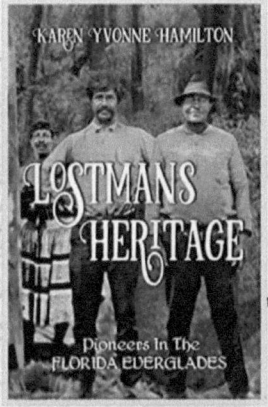

Everglades Pioneers

The men and women who settled in the Florida Everglades before the Civil War thrived in an environment that was dangerous and wild and ever changing. While others came and went, the pioneers faced every challenge nature and man threw at them and carried on. They may have migrated from island to island now and again, but the Everglades were their home. And they did what they had to do to survive.

About the Book

Lostmans Heritage follows the author's journey as she searches for her ancestors from the slave country of Savannah to the wilds of the Florida Everglades. Her story begins with her ancestor, Richard Hamilton, who was first introduced to the world in Peter Matthiessen's novel, *Killing Mr. Watson*. Richard untangled himself from the bonds of slavery and began a family and a life in the Ten Thousand Islands. Hamilton's research follows Richard and other Everglades residents to the ending of an era when the National Park Service took over the islands. Along the way Hamilton uncovers secrets and stories, polygamy, bootlegging, fist fights, murders, gangsters, killers, and tales of tomahawks and missing schoolteachers.

LOSTMANS HERITAGE: PIONEERS OF THE FLORIDA EVERGLADES
Author: Karen Yvonne Hamilton
Category: Nonfiction
Format: 6x9 Paperback
ISBN: 9781698126548
Pages: 213

Hamilton lives in Jupiter, Florida and is available for presentations and interviews.
kyvonnehamilton@gmail.com
Tel. 772.882.8582

www.yesterdaypress.com

"Probably the most historically accurate book about old Southwest Florida I've read...."

About the Author

KAREN YVONNE HAMILTON has spent the past 30 years researching her family history and life in the Everglades. Her educational background includes a BA in English and credits towards an MFA in Creative Writing. She spent two years actively immersed in research, interviews, and forays to the islands. Hamilton has published essays with Heritage Press, Florida Living, and the St. Pauls Review, and was a finalist in the 2017 New Letters Award in Creative Nonfiction. For over 20 years, she has facilitated workshops on creative writing, genealogy, and Florida history in her community and online.

"...deeply researched and a fascinating read."

www.yesterdaypress.com

www.ingramcontent.com/pod-product-compliance
Lightning Source LLC
Chambersburg PA
CBHW030853170426
43193CB00009BA/595